FLORA BRITANNICA BOOK OF
SPRING FLOWERS

FLORA BRITANNICA BOOK OF

SPRING
FLOWERS

RICHARD MABEY

Supported by Common Ground

With photographs by
Bob Gibbons and Gareth Lovett Jones

CHATTO & WINDUS
London

First published 1998

© Richard Mabey 1998

Richard Mabey has asserted his right under the
Copyright, Designs and Patents Act 1988 to be
identified as the author of this work

First published in the United Kingdom in 1998
by Chatto & Windus
Random House, 20 Vauxhall Bridge Road,
London SW1V 2SA

Random House Australia (Pty) Limited
20 Alfred Street, Milsons Point, Sydney,
New South Wales 2061, Australia

Random House New Zealand Limited
18 Poland Road, Glenfield,
Auckland 10, New Zealand

Random House South Africa (Pty) Limited
Endulini, 5A Jubilee Road, Parktown 2193,
South Africa

Random House UK Limited Reg. No. 954009

A CIP catalogue record for this book is available
from the British Library

Papers used by Random House UK Limited are
natural, recyclable products made from wood
grown in sustainable forests. The manufacturing
processes conform to the environmental
regulations of the country of origin.

ISBN 1–85619–728–X

Design by Ian Muggeridge

Printed and bound in Singapore
by Tien Wah Press

CONTENTS

INTRODUCTION

THE SPRING is the flower world's crowning moment. Indeed, the opening of flowers is a major part of the definition of spring. Botanists even have a measure of the advance of the season across the land, based on the time common and widespread flowers first come into bloom. Different species flower at times determined by a combination of daylight length and temperature, and in general bloom later the higher and further north they are. The lines joining points where a given species blooms on the same day are called isophenes, and from them it is possible to calculate that spring travels north and inland at roughly two miles per hour – very close to strolling pace! But the surfaces of Britain are so intimately convoluted that at a local level the principle breaks down. Spring flowering remains an intensely local affair, celebrated nationally, but with a different focus in every wood and parish.

The contents of this volume are concerned with our diverse responses to the spring, and derive from contributions made to *Flora Britannica*, a nationwide project to determine where wild plants stand in our cultural, social and domestic lives – whether, in short, we still have a living botanical folklore.

In Britain, wild plants have traditionally had a central role in folklore. We pick sprigs of heather for luck, munch blackberries in autumn, remember Wordsworth's famous lines when the wild daffodils are in flower, and link hands around threatened trees. Our children still make daisy chains, whack conkers and stick goosegrass stems on each other's backs. Despite being one of the most industrialised and urbanised countries on earth, we cling to plant rituals and mystical gestures whose roots stretch back into prehistory: holly decoration for the winter solstice, kisses under the mistletoe, the wearing of red poppies to commemorate the casualties of war. We name our houses, streets and settlements after plants, and use them as the most prolific source of decorative motifs on everything from stained glass to serviettes. From the outside, it must look as if

The colony of wild daffodils that Wordsworth commemorated in his poem 'I wandered lonely as a cloud ...' still survives on the banks of Ullswater in the Lake District.

we are botanical aboriginals, still in thrall to the spirits of vegetation.

But is this just the dying stages of an obstinate habit, the outward signs of a longing for the rural life that most of us have lost, or is it something deeper? Do we really still believe in the bad luck that may-blossom can bring into a house, and in the efficacy of the increasing numbers of herbal nostrums crowding onto our chemists' shelves? Or is our seeming respect now a touch tongue-in-cheek? When wild flowers are dragged willy-nilly into shampoo advertisements and state rituals, maybe it is time to ask whether the particular plants themselves have any meanings left for us, or whether they have become purely notional, registers of a fashionably Green 'life-style'.

When the survey work on *Flora Britannica* started, this was the question that underpinned all others. We were aware of surviving crafts and cottage wisdom, and of the familiarity expressed in our immense legacy of vernacular plant names. What we did not know was whether, as a people (or collection of peoples), we could be said to have an intimacy with plants that was more than purely nostalgic and backward-looking. Did people still meet under meeting-place trees? Were children inventing new names and games for the new, exotic species constantly escaping into the wild, as they did centuries ago, say, for horse-chestnut and sycamore seeds? And was that two-way traffic of wild and cultivated plants over the garden wall still busy? Did plants continue to play any role in our senses of place and season, those fundamental aspects of everyday life that seem everywhere to be under threat from regimentation and the ironing out of local differences? How had the attractions of wild food and native herbal remedies survived into the era of convenience food and prescription medicines?

These were the kind of questions which were asked when *Flora Britannica* was launched in the winter of 1991–2. Over the four years that followed, the project was regularly publicised on television and in the press, as well as through schools, community groups and amenity societies (more than a hundred of these at local and national levels). The many thousands of responses came in all manner of forms – postcards, tapes of discussions, snapshots and family reminiscences, as well as long and detailed essays on the botanical folklore of individual parishes and individual species.

Those contributions which discussed the plants of spring and our responses to and feelings about them form the backbone of this current book.

A note on the text

The text includes species of flowering plants from England, Scotland and Wales. Ireland and the Channel Isles are not included. The species are to some extent self-selected by whether they have figured in local culture and whether contributors reported this. By British botanical standards there is an unusual number of introduced and naturalised species, which are often found more interesting and which, of course, began with a cultural profile, often by already being in trade or in cultivation.

The vernacular names (indicated as 'VN') are all ones that were contributed to the project as being in current use, and they are normally printed in the spellings in which they were submitted. I have tried to eliminate obvious copying from previous printed sources, though there are inevitably some borderline cases. Except in special circumstances, I have not indicated particular areas where particular names prevail. The geographical mobility of contributors, who are often writing from one place and remembering another, and the mobility of the names themselves through the mass media, would have made this a misleading and potentially inaccurate qualification.

The notes from contributors are printed as they were sent in. Editing has been confined to selection of passages and occasional changes in spelling and punctuation to assist clarity. Editorial additions are indicated by square brackets. As many of the contributions were handwritten, I must apologise if I have made any errors of transcription either in the text itself or in the names of contributors.

Reference numbers refer to the Source notes section, which starts on page 136. Contributors are referred to in this section by name, parish and county.

Woods

Woods are the sites of the earliest spring flowers for a very simple and fundamental biological reason: woodland plants, needing sunlight like all others, are adapted to go through their most intense period of growth before the leaf canopy in the trees above them closes. So, beginning often in late January with spurge-laurel and naturalised snowdrops, we see in

March wood anemones, violets and primroses; and in April bluebells, early-purple orchid and wild garlic. By mid-summer the leaves of many of the spring lilies have died away, to be replaced by ranker plants such as hogweed, stinging nettle and rosebay willowherb.

Bluebells in 'Devil's Churchyard' wood, near Checkendon, Oxfordshire.

Stinking hellebore, *Helleborus foetidus*, is a perennial of woods and scrub on calcium-rich soils, with lime-green flowers edged with claret and held in sprays above stiff, fingered, evergreen leaves from late January till May. The southern chalk-hills are the place to see it, where the flowers glow amongst tangled hazel shoots and the dark foliage of yew and holly. This is where the eighteenth-century naturalist Gilbert White knew it, in the hanging woods above Selborne in Hampshire (where it still flourishes). He thought it 'very ornamental in shady walks and shrubberies' and transplanted it to his garden. He also noted that the local women 'give the leaves powdered to children troubled with worms', but that it was a 'violent remedy'.[1] There is some clue to this in the smell, not stinking exactly but reminiscent of the unpleasant mousy tang of hemlock.

Left: stinking hellebore stays evergreen even in the hardest winters.

Nonetheless 'setterwort' has remained a garden favourite (though most plants come from continental stock these days) and has become naturalised some way beyond its natural range. A yellow-foliaged form that has occurred in the wild in three different sites recently looks a likely garden plant of the future.[2]

Green hellebore, *H. viridis*, has a similar range and taste in habitats. It is a less spectacular plant, with dull green flowers and sprawling, jagged leaves which die back in winter. But it can often form quite large colonies. The species most often planted out in gardens, *H. orientalis*, the **Lenten-rose**, is naturalised here and there in southern England.

Winter aconite, known as 'choirboys' in Suffolk.

Winter aconite, *Eranthis hyemalis*, from southern Europe, is often the very first flower to bloom in gardens in

Wood anemones, flowering in old woodland in early spring, before the leaf canopy closes.

mid-January, and is widely naturalised in plantations, road-sides and churchyards. The yellow flowers have been called 'choirboys' in Suffolk, from the ruffs that surround them.[3]
Love-in-a-mist, *Nigella damascena*, escapes occasionally to waste ground and rubbish-tips.

Wood anemone, *Anemone nemorosa* (VN: Windflower, Grandmother's nightcap, Moggie nightgown). Wood anemone is one of the earliest spring flowers, and one of the most faithful indicators of ancient woodland. Its seed in Britain is rarely fertile and, even when it is, does not stay viable for long. Instead, the plant spreads at a snail's pace – no more than six feet each hundred years – through the growth of its root structure.[4] Wood anemone is consequently a very confined plant, rarely extending its territory beyond its anciently traditional sites. These are usually in long-established woodland, though in the West Country it is also abundant in hedge-banks. Elsewhere it is frequent in ancient meadowland; and in the Yorkshire Dales, for instance, in limestone pavements. In many of these places the colonies may be relics of previous woodland cover, but the windflower's liking for light suggests that it may not be a plant of purely woodland origins. It will not grow in deep shade and opens its blooms fully only in sunshine.

On warm days in early April, a large colony of anemones can fill the air with a sharp, musky smell, which is hinted at in some of the old local names such as 'smell foxes'. Most of these names are now obsolete, but there are at least two comparatively new ones – 'moggie nightgown' in parts of Derbyshire ('In Stanley Common a "moggie" is a mouse, not a cat'[5]) and the delightful, if not especially appropriate, children's mis-hearing, 'wooden enemies'.

Colonies of wood anemones with purple or purple-streaked petals are quite frequent, e.g. in Wayland Wood, Norfolk, the site of the Babes in the Wood legend. But the sky-blue form, var. *caerulea*, is much rarer, and may have been lost. It was a great favourite of the nineteenth-century pioneer of 'wild gardening', William Robinson, who was careful to distinguish it from the occasionally naturalised European **blue anemone**, *A. apennina*:
'The most beautiful form of our wood Anemone … is the large sky-blue form. I first saw it as a small tuft in Oxford, and grew it in London where it was often seen with me in

bloom by Mr Boswell Syme, author of the Third Edition of Sowerby,[6] who had a great love for plants in a living state as well as in their merely "botanical" aspects, and we were often struck with its singular charm about noon on bright days. There is reason to believe that there is both in England and Ireland a large and handsome form of the wood Anemone – distinct from the common white of our woods and shaws in spring, and that my blue Anemone is a variety of this. It is not the same as the blue form wild in parts of North Wales and elsewhere in Britain, this being more fragile looking and not so light a blue.'[7]

The violets are a variable and promiscuous family, apt to throw up all kinds of sports and hybrids. For the first fifty years of this century botanists – fonder in those days of 'splitting' than 'lumping' species – responded in kind, and dutifully logged every slight variation. In the Revd Keble Martin's loving and meticulous account of the flora of Devon (1939) – a county abundant with violets – there are some 40 species, crosses, forms, colour oddities, eccentric shapes and local varieties, including one delectable type found only in the villages of Marldon, Berry Pomeroy and Dartington, *Viola odorata* var. *variegata*: 'This colour-variety may be distinguished from var. *dumetorum* in having its white petals irregularly splashed and streaked with violet, whereas in *dumetorum* the reverse of the upper petals is coloured to a greater or less degree with reddish purple.'[8] By 1948, when the Revd H. J. Riddelsdell's copious Gloucestershire Flora appeared, the roll-call of violet types had risen to 50, including no fewer than 18 varieties of the hairy violet, *V. hirta*, and an intriguing form *leucantha* of the early dog-violet, *V. reichenbachiana*, from Pighole near Tidenham: 'A considerable colony of pure white flowers, many spurless; and then looking very much like the flowers of *Oxalis acetosella* [wood-sorrel]!'[9]

Clive Stace's *New Flora of the British Isles* (1993) prunes this wildly proliferating catalogue (and maybe a little of its glamour too) down to a mere 28 species, subspecies and hybrids. The following are some of the best known and most interesting:

Common dog-violet, *V. riviniana*, is the commonest and most widespread species, flowering in deciduous woods, hedge-banks and old pastures from April to June.

The flowers are unscented (hence 'dog' violet, to distinguish it from the scented 'sweet' species), variable in colour and often rather stumpy. It was almost certainly this species that John Clare wrote of in his little-known poem 'Holywell'. Most violet poetry is little more than purple poesy, and it is a relief to read the sympathetic and unornamented clarity of Clare's vision:

Common dog-violet, Lincolnshire.

And just to say that spring was come,
The violet left its woodland home,
And, hermit-like, from storms and wind
Sought the best shelter it could find,
'Neath long grass banks, with feeble flowers
Peeping faintly purple flowers.[10]

Early dog-violet, *V. reichenbachiana*, is a slightly more petite species, with a preference for ancient woodlands, not occurring much outside England and normally in bloom by March. Both these two species of woodland violet can respond rampantly when light is allowed into a wood. In Hayley Wood in Cambridgeshire a forty-fold increase in the number of violet flowers has been recorded after coppicing.[11]

Sweet violet, *V. odorata*, prefers rather more open habitats, in hedges and scrub as well as woods. It is a native species, although many colonies are obvious escapes from cultivation, especially those in churchyards and on village greens and banks. It is easily recognised by its large, hairy, pale green, heart-shaped leaves and tufted habit. The flowers may be deep bluish, purple, white, even cream; but the rich-red form (Riddelsdell's var. *rubro-purpurea*) is rare, and was understandably the favourite plant of one Bedfordshire woman: 'My mother's most specific botanical memory is of a red violet that used to grow inside a gateway of a grass field between Rushden and Newton Bromswold. I suspect it was a colour variant of the sweet violet.'[12]

The fragrance of the *V. odorata* flowers can be very strong and they have been used in the making of perfume as far back as Classical Greece. (The scent can seem to be curiously fleeting, though this is a phenomenon of our sense of smell, not the flower. One of the chemicals contributing to the scent of violets is ionine, which has the ability temporarily to deaden the smell receptors that detect it.) In medieval Britain sweet violets were one of the strewing herbs used as early household deodorants. They also had a role in herbal medicine, especially for insomnia, headache and depression. And they led John Gerard to say some wise words about the more subtle, psychosomatic healing effects of plants. He wrote that
'the blacke or purple Violets, or March Violets of the Garden, … haue a great prerogatiue aboue others, not onely bicause the minde conceiueth a certaine pleasure and recreation by smelling and handling of these most odoriferous flowers, but also for that very many by these Violets receiue ornament and comely grace: for there be made of them Garlands for the heade, nosegaies and poesies, which are delightfull to looke on and pleasant to

smell to, speaking nothing of their appropriate vertues; yea Gardens themselues receiue by these the greatest ornament of all, chiefest beautie, and most gallant grace; and the recreation of the minde which is taken heereby, cannot be but verie good and honest: for they admonish & stir vp a man to that which is comely & honest.'[13]

Heath dog-violet, *V. canina*, is normally pale blue, with a cream-coloured spur, and quite common on grassy heaths and fens on sandy, acid soils. **Hairy violet**, *V. hirta*, is rather similar to the early dog-violet, but covered with short hairs, and preferring open habitats on calcareous soils. The flowers are normally a conventional violet colour, but can vary from white to slate-grey.

Teesdale violet, *V. rupestris*, is a famous local rarity from short-turfed limestone pastures in the northern Pennines and Cumbria. Much of the population that grows on the crumbly 'sugar limestone' of Upper Teesdale in Durham was destroyed when the Cow Green reservoir was built on the site at the end of the 1960s. It is a dwarf, tufted plant, with roundish flowers in shades of white, pale blue or reddish violet. **Fen violet**, *V. persicifolia*, is an even rarer species, confined recently to just two fenland sites in Cambridgeshire, Woodwalton Fen and Wicken Fen, both now National Nature Reserves. To judge from its previous much wider distribution and its favoured haunts in Ireland, the fen violet is a short-lived perennial with very fussy habitat needs: short, damp calcareous turf which is subject to win-

Teesdale violet, a rarity restricted to short-turfed limestone pastures in the north.

ter flooding and periodically grazed or disturbed in some
way to help distribute its seed. The blooms are perhaps the
most beautiful of all the native violets, the mottled bluish-
white flowers often suffused with a mother-of-pearl sheen.

Pansies are as muddled – and muddling – a group as the
violets proper. The most frequent species, the little **field
pansy**, *V. arvensis*, is becoming increasingly common as an
annual weed of arable and disturbed ground. On set-aside
land and newly made road-verges, its long-stalked flowers
can be found winding amongst the grasses in almost any
month of the year. They are variable in size and usually pale
yellow in colour, but are often suffused or blotched with
purple, especially on the upper 'ears' or in streaks in the
'eye'. (Pansies, more than any other native species, have
blooms which are irresistibly reminiscent of 'faces' – as
many of the obsolete names testify, e.g. three-faces-under-a-
hood, cat's face.) Occasionally the whole flower is violet.
These multicoloured forms can be difficult to tell from the
wild pansy, *V. tricolor* (VN: Heartsease) – especially as this
hybridises with *V. arvensis*, and throws up plenty of colour

*Field and wild
pansies, drawn by
Caroline May in
1834 and 1842,
showing the
variation that was
exploited in
cultivation.*

variants of its own. As the Latin name indicates, there are often three different shades on each bloom – most commonly violet, yellow and blue, but also reddish-purple, rusty-red, white or an almost blackish, velvety blue. They can also be pure yellow, or pure purple. One mid-May, on Barnham Cross Common in Norfolk, I found sheets of heartsease of both colours – and of most possible combinations between – growing on a patch of sandy soil that had been scorched by a fire the year before. These may have been the subspecies *curtisii*, which normally grows on coastal sand-dunes but also on the inland sands of East Anglia's Breckland (especially on firebreaks). A few miles to the east, a householder found other forms taking more unconventional advantage of environmental change: 'In Harleston, south Norfolk, during the recession, wherever there were For Sale notices and run-down lawns, there were purple heartsease in hundreds. They love the sandy soils here.'[14] *V. tricolor* is a species which can grow both as an annual and as a short-lived perennial, and colonise grassland on acid soils as well as cultivated ground. In Derbyshire and central Wales it begins to overlap with the southern outposts of the mountain pansy, and yet more intriguing liaisons begin …

The **mountain pansy**, *V. lutea*, is a squat, vivacious plant, and its exquisite flowers, normally pale yellow, are held on stiff stalks that seem to spring straight from the turf. On hill pastures you can sometimes see acres of them shivering in the wind. In Shropshire, for instance, 'in the 1940s, it was still possible to walk from Ratlinghope via Squilver and Shelve to Bromlow Callow through field after field washed with mountain pansies'.[15] Here, as in many other places, they have declined because of agricultural pressure. But, in general, the mountain pansy is a resilient plant. It will tolerate quite heavy grazing, and enjoys soils with a high mineral content – even lead spoil-tips. Where it occurs on limestone soils (as in the Derbyshire and Yorkshire Dales) it is usually in areas where rainfall has leached out the calcium carbonate and left other minerals behind.[16]

Like other *Viola* species it is highly variable in colour and form. Many of the Scottish colonies are var. *amoena*, which is entirely purple save for some yellow streaking around the 'eye'. A magnificent form of this – deep purple and an inch

across – grows on Ben Lawers on Tayside. Forms with pur-
plish ears grow in high Teesdale hay-meadows, often mixed
with *V. tricolor*. In grasslands on the banks of the River
Tyne in Northumberland, the two species unquestionably
cross (the seeds of the *V. lutea* travelling down-river to meet
the more lowland *V. tricolor*) and form spectacularly variegated hybrid swarms: 'These are our special glory, growing
in sheets in fields and clearings near the river. Colours vary,
in every possible combination of blue, purple, white and
yellow.'[17]

It is the tendency of the pansy tribe to be naturally
'sportive' that spurred the early cultivators into action in the
mid-nineteenth century. The first garden varieties were
raised simply by progressively selecting the most interesting
chance seedlings from the various forms and crosses of *V.
tricolor* and *V. arvensis*. Then William Thompson, Lord
Gambier's gardener at Iver in Buckinghamshire, added
strains of *V. tricolor* from Holland to the breeding stock,
and produced the first all-blue variety. There followed the
famous 'Beauty of Iver', which had a broad 'face' of pure
yellow, encircled by an edge of sky-blue.

Meanwhile James Grieve of Edinburgh was breeding
violas, using as his starting point our native mountain pan-

*Mountain pansies
from Perthshire,
showing the
extremes of colour
variation.
Intermediates and
blooms with
blotched 'eyes' and
'ears' are common.*

sies and the pert, long-stalked, blue- or white-flowered **horned pansy**, *V. cornuta*, from the Pyrenees (which is naturalised in some places in Britain). The road to the vast array of modern garden pansies had been opened.[18] Conventionally these are now lumped together under the scientific tag of *Viola × wittrockiana*, which is believed to contain genes from all our native species. It frequently self-seeds or escapes into open and waste places, and, it hardly needs to be added, is already back-crossing with its parents.

Coralroot, *Cardamine bulbifera*, is a scarce and very local species of old deciduous woodland with a strangely disjointed distribution. Genuinely wild colonies occur in two quite distinct and widely separated regions: the wet, acid woodlands of the Weald in Kent and Sussex, and the drier, usually more calcareous Chiltern beechwoods. (There is a third, possibly native cluster, around Needwood Forest in Staffordshire.)

Coralroot is one of the most subtly beautiful woodland

Coralroot, a very local species of old woodland in the Chilterns and the Weald.

plants, its soft, pale lilac flowers held on stalks a foot or 18 inches high and coming into bloom at the same time as, and often amongst, the bluebells. It has been widely introduced into woodland gardens, where it often becomes naturalised. There are, for instance, established colonies in the well-known gardens at Knightshayes Court and Dartington Hall, both in Devon, at Cliveden in Buckinghamshire, and in Ellen Willmott's old garden at Warley Place in Essex.

Coralroot spreads both by the extension of its root net-work and by means of the little purple-brown bulbils that lie between leaves and stem. These are easily dislodged from the plant by birds or strong winds, from June onwards. Given these twin means of reproduction it is a little surprising that the plant hasn't escaped more often from its garden strongholds. But there are feral colonies in, for example, Smallcombe Wood, Bath; a small hornbeam copse near Wellingore Hall Park, Lincolnshire; woodland at Silverdale, Lancashire (naturalised from an adjoining nursery); and Scalby Churchyard, Yorkshire, where it has been since at least 1900, and 'since it reached the wall of the churchyard it has not looked back'.[19]

Wild cherry, *Prunus avium* (VN: Gean, Mazzard, Murry). The wild cherry is arguably the most seasonally ornamental of our native woodland trees. The drifts of delicate white blossom are often out in early April, just before the leaves, while in autumn its leaves turn a fiery mix of yellow and crimson. Even the bark – peeling to reveal dark, shiny-red patches – is extravagantly colourful for a British tree.

Cherry is a tree of the southern half of Britain and prefers chalky soils, even though it will grow on acid plateaux, as in the Chilterns. This is one of its favourite areas, and it can form large colonies by its vigorous and pro-lific suckers. When these are at the edges of woods, as they often are (cherry needs light to regenerate), they can make the entire wood seem to be ringed with white at blossom-time. A couple of weeks later, when the flowers have fallen, the woods are ringed again, on the ground. After the great storms of October 1987 and January 1990, there was another cherry delight the following spring: windblown trees blooming horizontally in the woods, like flowering hedges. In Fingest, in the south Chilterns, gean blossom is used to decorate the church at Eastertide.[20]

Cherry blossom at dusk in the Chilterns.

Wood-sorrel, *Oxalis acetosella* (VN: Alleluia, Cuckoo's bread and cheese, Granny's sour grass). Wood-sorrel, whose delicate, veined, white flowers usually appear between Easter and Whitsun, has long been called Alleluia, a plant which joins in the celebration of the Resurrection and Ascension.[21] But it was left to the Victorians to tease religious meanings out of its minutest habits. Charlotte Clifford, one of the family responsible for *The Frampton Flora*,[22] copied into her diary for 1860 a passage on the species from *The Garland of the Year*. This was a popular botanical annual at the time, and the passage is an extravagant but typical example of the contemporary custom of

using the lives of plants (well observed, it must be granted)
as moral parables:
'A more beautiful floral emblem of praise could not be
selected than this exquisitely sensitive little plant. Coming
forth at the first summons of spring it continues to adorn
the woods with its bright triple leaves, until the fading
foliage of autumn consigns it to a living grave. Even then,
the flower-searcher may discover here and there a
delicately-folded leaf looking out from the desolation and
death by which it is surrounded. For the alleluya, fragile
though it be, can brave the roughest gales, and weather the
wildest storms, bowing its meek head beneath the clouds,

and looking up with joy, to greet the sunshine. Sweet and precious are the lessons which this little woodland plant may teach us – lessons of humble faith, and constant loving praise. Teaching us that, as the shrinking wood sorrel finds protection in its triple leaves, so our souls, strengthened by the three-fold gifts of the Holy Ghost, should bow in meek submission to the trials of their mortal existence. Ever praising, never repining, bearing all sorrow; thankful for all joys!'

Wood-sorrel, blooming around Eastertime and popularly known in much of Europe as 'alleluia'.

The trefoil, shamrock-shaped leaves are wood-sorrel's most distinctive feature. They lie in layered clumps in shady woods and hedge-banks, often growing directly on leaf-mould or cushioned by moss on fallen logs. When they first open they can look an almost luminous viridian, and they are folded back (their religious associations seemingly inexhaustible) like an episcopal hat. Then they open flat, three hearts with their points joined at the stem. Gerard Manley Hopkins thought they were like 'green lettering', but their symmetrical clusters have more of the look of fretwork.

As might be guessed from its other surviving names, wood-sorrel has been used as a green vegetable, though it is slightly toxic if eaten in large quantities. The sour, lemon-sharp leaves are reminiscent of sorrel, *Rumex acetosa*. John Evelyn recommended them as a salad.[23] One forager from Lancashire adds them to cream-cheese sandwiches.[24]

Colour variants are sometimes found. A deep pink form has been seen near Abbey St Bathans in Berwickshire, and a purple in Torver, Cumbria.[25]

Moschatel, *Adoxa moschatellina* (VN: Townhall clock, Good Friday plant). An inconspicuous but delightful plant of woods and shady banks, moschatel is one of the first spring flowers to come into bloom, nearly always by the beginning of April (hence 'Good Friday plant'). The small flowers are pale yellowish-green in colour, but are arranged in a remarkable fashion, at right angles to one another, like the faces of a town clock – except that there is a fifth on top, pointing towards the sky. At the end of the war, when I was a small child, I was told this was 'for the Spitfire pilots to read'.

Townhall clock often grows in quite large colonies, especially where the soil is damp or slightly disturbed, as along the edges of woodland rides. On warm damp days

(or simply sniffed close-to) the massed flowers give off a faint but memorable scent of musk.

Fritillary, *Fritillaria meleagris* (VN: Snake's-head, Snake's-head lily, Crowcups, Frawcups, Leper's bells, Sulky ladies, Chequered lily, Folfalarum). The snake's-head fritillary is one of the most local of well-known British flowers, and one of the most darkly glamorous. Vita Sackville-West wrote of it in her epic pastoral poem 'The Land':

Moschatel, whose flowers are arranged like the faces of a cube or a townhall clock. They smell faintly of musk.

> *And then I came to a field where the springing grass*
> *Was dulled by the hanging cups of fritillaries,*
> *Sullen and foreign-looking, the snaky flower,*
> *Scarfed in dull purple, like Egyptian girls*
> *Camping among the furze, staining the waste*
> *With foreign colour, sulky-dark and quaint ...*[26]

But it has not been exclusively a poet's plant. Across southern and middle England, a flamboyant suite of local names – snake's-head in Oxfordshire, leper's lily in Somerset, shy widows in Warwickshire, for instance – suggested a flower that was once widespread and familiar. The anonymous namers had really *seen* those dusky, reptilian bells, with their checkered patches of mulberry and lilac seeming to overlap like scales. Even up to the 1930s the fritillary grew in its thousands in more than a hundred 10-km squares, yet always locally enough, in winter-flooded hay meadows, to be intimately known and cherished. Some individual villages in Wiltshire even had their own names for it. In Oaksey it was the Oaksey lily; in Minety, the Minety bell. It was florid, profuse, extraordinary, intensely local.

Yet the first official record of a wild fritillary in England was not made, remarkably, until 1736, and this has made it top of the list of those species whose origins have been a source of nagging curiosity amongst botanists, sometimes to the exclusion of more intriguing aspects of its social and cultural history. Is it a native? A Roman introduction? An escapee, as Geoffrey Grigson believed, from Tudor gardens?[27]

In the two and a half centuries since that first 'discovery', the fritillary has come and gone with frightening speed, its distribution savagely cut by agricultural drainage and development from 27 counties before the last war to roughly the same number of individual meadows today. But it has remained, in the best sense, a parochial plant, best glimpsed through the stories of its changing fortunes in its surviving strongholds.

It was certainly about in English gardens by the sixteenth century. Gerard calls it the 'checkered Daffodill or Ginny hen flower ... in so much that euery leafe [i.e. petal] seemeth to be the feather of a Ginnie hen' and '*Frittillaria*, of the table or boord vpon which men plaie at chesse, which square checkers the flower doth very much resemble', and he remarks that 'Of the faculties of these pleasant flowers there is nothing set downe in ancient or later writers, but are greatly esteemed for the beautifieng of our gardens, and the bosomes of the beautifull.'[28]

Philip Oswald, who has reviewed most of the writings on the fritillary in Britain,[29] thinks that the first wild record may possibly post-date Gerard's note by about only 50 years. In his manuscript for *The Natural History of Wiltshire*, John Aubrey (1626–97) wrote: 'In a ground of mine called Swices ... growes abundantly a plant called by the people hereabout crow-bells, which I never saw any where but there.' 'Crow-bell' has been a vernacular name for a number of common wild flowers, including bluebell and buttercup. But Aubrey would have known these plants, and, given the location of his estate on the upper reaches of the Avon in Kington St Michael, Wiltshire, and other vernacular names for fritillary such as 'crowcup', Oswald thinks it just possible that he was referring to fritillaries.

But the accepted first record is the one of 1736. On 11 December that year, the botanist John Blackstone wrote to a friend that it 'grows in a meadow by a wood side near Harefield [Middlesex], and has done so about forty years as a neighbouring gentleman informs me'. In the following year he published what is presumably the same record: 'In Maud-fields near Ruislip Common, observed above forty years by Mr Ashby of Brakspears.' [10] The fritillaries had vanished from Maud Fields by the end of the eighteenth century. But, in 1990, the Ruislip and District Natural History Society obtained permission from the current owner of the land to plant out 2,000 bulbs (obtained from a commercial nursery, not a wild source). So far, the survival rate has not been good, though some of the plants appear to be dividing and seeding successfully.

The best-known fritillary site in England is probably Magdalen College Meadow in Oxford, where in late April the entire north-eastern half of the meadow seems covered by a tremulous purple haze. Yet, curiously for a university city devoted to scholarship and science, this spectacular display just a few hundred yards from the oldest Botanic Garden in Britain, was not even *spotted* by botanists until 1785, when it was recorded by John Lightfoot. A century later George Claridge Druce remarked: 'It was not a little singular that the Fritillary, so conspicuous a plant of the Oxford meadows, should have so long remained unnoticed by the various botanists who had resided in or visited Oxfordshire.' Perhaps 'unnoticed by ... *botanists*' is the key. In Middlesex, it was first reported by a non-botanist, Blackstone's grandfather, Francis Ashby. By contrast, at Oxford, the Professor of Botany at the time that the Magdalen colony was belatedly 'discovered' was Humphrey Sibthorp, a man of such renowned indolence that he reputedly gave just one not very successful lecture in forty years. The men of books and laboratories were not always the most energetic and sharpest of eye in the field.

And it is just possible that the Magdalen colony was

an introduction from another, more convincingly wild, Oxfordshire site. About six miles west of the city is the village of Ducklington, in the Windrush Valley. This has long had fritillaries growing in its low-lying meadowland, and in the eighteenth century the living of its church was under the patronage of Magdalen College. It has been suggested that

Fritillaries in a 1934 window at Ducklington church, Oxfordshire. 'Fritillary Sunday' is still kept up in the village.

Fritillaries at first light, Magdalen College Meadow, Oxford.

an incumbent at Ducklington may have taken a fancy to the flowers and carried some bulbs back to his college to plant.[31] (There is a similarity between the two populations in that both have a high proportion of plants with pure white blooms.) They have certainly been in Ducklington 'beyond living memory':

'The field by the River Windrush used to flood regularly when the water table was higher. Local residents remember the fields looking purple, even black with them. The flowers used to be sent to Covent Garden, and local children used to go to Birmingham to sell fritillary posies. After the war, the water table was lowered and arable crops sown on all available fields, except for one which was purchased by Roger Peel, who lives in the Manor. It now belongs to his two sons, who own it jointly but do not live locally: it has been taken over by the local community and is legally tied up so it can't be sold except to the National Trust. Once a year on Fritillary Sunday [late April or early May] the field is open to the public.'[32]

There are many representations of fritillaries in the church, though mostly twentieth-century. They appear in a stained-glass window dating from 1934, ornament a 1973 embroidered altar frontal and pew cushions, and are carved in a semi-formal chaplet on the pulpit (where they were previously misidentified as tulips, perhaps because 'wild tulips' was once a local name for the flower). The pulpit originally came from Magdalen College. There is also a framed photograph hanging in the church of a remarkable fritillary with pale lemon flowers.

The celebration of the flower, including the holding of a 'Fritillary Sunday', when flowers can be picked (or simply admired) in return for collections for charities, has been going on in many sites for at least a century. Iffley Meadow was one of Oxfordshire's traditional picking sites, and children could reputedly sell posies of the flowers in Oxford High Street provided they were more than nine years old.[33] Iffley's fritillaries vary enormously in numbers, but probably more as a result of weather and winter flooding than picking. In 1933 there were only two blooms. In 1987 numbers dropped to 300 when bad weather had made a hay-cut impossible the previous year. Since 1983, when the Berks, Bucks and Oxon Naturalists' Trust took over the management of the meadow and began an annual and far from solemn count of blooms, the number has crept above 12,000 in both 1992 and 1994.

Iffley is one of the sites that was known to Matthew Arnold, who wrote about fritillaries in his poem 'Thyrsis':

I know what white, what purple fritillaries
The grassy harvest of the river-fields,
Above by Ensham, down by Sandford, yields;
And what sedged brooks are Thames's tributaries.

To the south-west, by some smaller tributaries of the Thames, snake's-heads survive on the Duke of Wellington's estate at Stratfield Saye. These meadows are still opened to the public (just for looking) when the fritillaries are in flower. But before the last war, the public were allowed to pick the blooms, as the poet Andrew Young has described: 'at a field-gate … a woman sat collecting money. Paying my pence I entered the field, maroon-coloured with the drooping heads of Fritillaries. People moved slowly about, stooping to pick those flowers that looked like repentant serpents. All was so unexpected and strange that I had the feeling I was in heaven; I was even troubled to think that I was not engaged like the others. Picking flowers seemed the only occupation in heaven.'[34]

To the east of Oxford, one of the largest and most famous Fritillary Sunday sites was in the parish of Dinton (previously spelt, though probably not pronounced, Donnington) near Ford, Buckinghamshire. The first suggestive record that there were fritillaries in the area appears on a privately commissioned map of the area dated 1803. On it there is a large plot labelled 'Frogcup Meadow'.[35] Grigson cites the similarly pronounced 'Frockup' as a vernacular name for the plant in Buckinghamshire, suggesting that this may mean either 'frog cup', deriving from fritillary's companion creatures in the meadow, or 'frock-cup', from the shape of the flowers.[36] (Less reverent commentators have suggested 'Frock-up', from human activities in the habitat.) But Leonard Bull, who lived in Ford for many years, has no doubts about the derivation of the name, which is, he says, properly 'Frawcup':
'The name Frawcup comes from the name of the hamlet,

White-flowered fritillaries are quite frequent in some populations.

Ford. This type of sound-change was a feature of the local dialect. Having been brought up in the area I could quote other similar examples, perhaps one which is still heard is the pronunciation of the local surname Goodearl as Goodrule.

I remember very well the origin of the mistaken derivation of Frawcup. At the end of the First World War a number of teachers came into the district who had no knowledge whatever of the local dialect and its mode of development. It was these people who mistakenly assumed the name was a slovenly corruption of "frogcup" and unfortunately their opinion became accepted as being correct. We, as children, strongly objected (for which we received corporal punishment), as we knew it really meant Fordcup.' [37]

Another local man has described the history of Fritillary Sunday in the parish:
'As a lad, in 1927, I was first taken to the place where the snake's-heads grow, and each year, with the odd exception or two, made the pilgrimage right up to 1939. Local custom made the second Sunday in May a special occasion on which a large number of people living around this area congregated at Ford to pick the snake's-heads. The snake's-head was (and is) locally called a Fraucup – Frodcup – Frawcup, and this particular Sunday was known as Fraucup Sunday.

[The meadows] were literally plastered with snake's-heads, hundreds of people picked great bunches, vying with each other as to who could pick the largest bunch. This picking did not seem to make any difference to the numbers growing each year; a lot of white forms were found, and on occasions twin-headed flowers, which were status symbols indeed.

A fence had been placed in the first hedge for people to enter, and a tin hung on it to receive donations to some charitable organisation, this tin was well filled with odd pence and ha'pence. Picnics were held among the flowers, and a great many cycles were parked by the roadside, and, as the years progressed, motor vehicles became more in evidence. Quite a few locals dug up plants, some of which or their progeny now grace some of our local gardens, orchards, lawns, etc.' [38]

A woman whose mother was brought up in Ford recalls that fritillaries also figured in local May Day celebrations: 'The children bound Fritillaries down the stem of Crown Imperial Lilies with grass and ribbon, making a pretty colourful wand. They then knocked on doors and chanted – "We've come to greet you because it's the first of May. Give us a penny then we'll run away." '[39]

Frogcup Meadow was ploughed up in the early 1950s, but a few fritillaries have clung on in a strip of damp commonland between the old meadow and the lane to Aston Mullins. I found three blooms in mid-April 1993, and met two local men who remembered the last of the Fritillary Sundays (which would have to be held in April nowadays to coincide with blooming). They confirmed the fact that several locals had taken bulbs before the meadow was destroyed. One of their neighbours' populations had increased from 25 to 250. I asked if this was in his garden, but was parried with consummate diplomacy by the reply, 'No, in a piece of ground'!

The most northern of the surviving sites for fritillaries in Britain is at Wheaton Aston in Staffordshire. They have been known here since 1787. In 1912, the local squire G. T. Hartley described them as: 'the black fields, where *Fritillaria* grow in considerable quantities ... On the first Sunday in May, an ancient wake known as Fritillary Wake, locally pronounced Falfillary, is held when people from all the villages around flock down to these moors to gather the flowers of two kinds – spotted Snakeshead and White.'[40]

Later 'Falfillary' became further corrupted to 'Folfalarum' – the '-arum' ending being quite a common suffix in vernacular English for words that are regarded as highfalutin.

Elsewhere in Staffordshire, a small population persists at Tamworth. They were rediscovered in Broad Meadow, by the River Tame, in 1958, when a local naturalist, George Arnold, found seven flowers. In recent years, the site has been managed by the Staffordshire Trust and, 'with a combination of propagation, secrecy and security', the number had increased to over 600 in 1990.[41]

At the beginning of this century, the fritillary also occurred widely in the river valleys of Suffolk, but it gradually disappeared as meadows were ploughed or drained.

One of the best, if smallest, was saved in 1938 at the very last minute: 'Part of the meadow had already been lightly ploughed, and a drainage ditch dug across the lower end …'[42] Mickfield is now a bewitching place, a small oasis of meadow flowers in a vast arable desert. There are also fritillaries at Rookery Farm, Monewden (now known as Martins Meadows), where they grow with wild daffodils, cowslips and orchids, and at 'Fox Meadow', Framsden. Here, again, there was a tradition of a Fritillary Sunday in aid of charity. The owner, 'Queenie' Fox, told the writer C. Henry Warren in the 1960s: 'A shilling – and everybody can take home a bunch of flowers … In aid of our local Cancer Fund … I think people *ought* to have a chance to see the fritillaries, don't you agree?'[43]

A few years later the meadow was sprayed with a broad-leaved weedkiller. But it was summertime, the fritillaries were leafless and they survived where almost all the other meadow flowers were obliterated. In 1978, the five-acre 'Fox Meadow' was acquired by the Suffolk Trust for Nature Conservation, and since then has been opened to the public for one day a year when the fritillaries are in bloom. But as wild flower festivals go, it is a depressing one, and symbolic of the change in the fritillary's status. The surviving flowers bloom in a tangle of rank grasses and thistles in a roped-off enclosure, round which the visitors slowly parade, as if they were at a botanical zoo.

To see fritillaries in immense abundance, you must go to North Meadow, in the Thames Valley at Cricklade, Wiltshire, where in a good year there may be several million in flower. North Meadow (now a National Nature Reserve) is an ancient common, and what is known as 'Lammas Land'. Its 44 acres are shut up for hay on 13 February each year until the hay harvest (apportioned by lot)[44] some time in July. On old Lammas Day, 12 August, it becomes the common pasture of the Borough of Cricklade, and any resident of the town may put up to ten head of horses or cattle on it, or (after 12 September) 20 head of sheep. As far as is known, this system of land tenure has continued unchanged for more than 800 years, and the show at North Meadow may be the best evidence that fritillary is a native species.

But its sheer abundance here has shown how an obsession with rarity can distort our sense of value. In 1978, just after the first Open Day at Fox Meadow, a national newspaper carried a large photograph of a clump of fritillaries at the site, mentioning its recent purchase but not its location. A TV news programme picked up the story and contacted the Nature Conservancy Council (NCC) about the possibility of getting a film of this rare and apparently secret plant. The NCC suggested that it was unlikely they would be given permission to make a private site so widely and explicitly public, but that they would be welcome to come and film fritillaries at the NCC's own North Meadow. But no sooner had the number of flowers been mentioned than the reporter lost interest. How could a plant growing with millions of its own kind be described as *rare*?[45]

Considering the concentration of surviving fritillary meadows along river systems of middle England, most botanists now consider that the species was a native in post-glacial England. On the continent its wild populations are concentrated around the flood plain of the Rhine, which, before the opening of the North Sea channel, about 5500 BC, formed part of a single river system embracing the Thames and many rivers in the Midlands and East Anglia. Fritillaries probably then grew naturally in seasonally flooded woodland clearings throughout this region. This, alas, is now virtually an extinct habitat in Britain. The one place you may see fritillaries growing under trees, in what is probably their natural habitat, is, with some poetic justice, the damp shrubberies around Magdalen Meadow in Oxford, where the plant's nativeness was first queried.

Solomon's-seal, *Polygonatum multiflorum*, is a remarkable plant to come across in a springtime copse, at any stage in its growth. Its early shoots are like narrow scrolls, which seem to expand telescopically until the full-grown stem is arching above the dog's mercury and ramsons. It can still be difficult to spot. The shelves of grey-green oval leaves are held parallel with the ground, catching the light only occasionally and obscuring the clusters of buttery white bell-flowers. Before these are fully open they are enough like teats to have earned the local Dorset name (now obsolete) of 'sow's tits'.

It is a local plant, concentrated in old woods (especially ash-woods) on the chalk in central southern England, though there are scattered colonies in limestone woods in

Solomon's-seal. Its rows of udder-like flowers gave it the nickname of 'sow's tits' in Dorset.

South Wales and the Lake District.

Herb-paris, *Paris quadrifolia*, is a cryptic and subtle woodland beauty. Above its four broad leaves, held flat like a Maltese cross, is a star of four very narrow yellow-green petals and four wider sepals, topped by a crown of eight golden stamens, and later a single shining black berry – the 'devil-in-a-bush' that was one of the plant's obsolete names.

The name 'paris' comes from the Latin *par*, meaning 'equal', and reflects this symmetry of the plant's parts, which also 'signed' the plant against the disorderly behaviour of witches and epileptics. But beyond its use in early herbalism, herb-paris, surprisingly, has almost no place in native folklore. This can't be altogether explained by its scarcity. Paris occurs in moist, woody places on calcareous soils through most of Britain, from Kent and Somerset up to

Banffshire. In the south it seems to prefer ancient woods –
in Wiltshire and Somerset on limestone, for instance, and in
Essex and Suffolk on boulder clay.

But on the Cotswold plateau it is spreading into young
deciduous plantations and self-sown woods. In Hampshire
it flourishes in some of the damp, hollow lanes and in
Derbyshire haunts streamside ash-woods. In the north-
west it will tolerate more rocky terrain, and in the Yorkshire
Dales it can sometimes be found marooned at the bottom of
fissures in limestone pavements. Paris will spread and
flower more freely when its favoured woods are thinned or

*Herb-paris, topped
by its striking
crown of eight
golden stamens, is a
plant of shady
woods on chalk or
limestone.*

coppiced. (It is the emblem of the recently formed Coppice Association.) But it is principally a plant of secluded, half-lit corners, and it is this, together with its muted coloration, that has made it such a private plant. In the dappled shade of a woodland floor in May its flat leaves often merge and overlap companion plants such as stinging nettle and dog's mercury. Searching for the clusters of even, oval leaves and for the dull glow of the golden antennae is one of the pleasures of hunting for herb-paris. Sometimes you will find plants with five leaves, and more unusually with three or six. In two woods in North Yorkshire plants with seven leaves have been found.[46] These asymmetrical varieties have always held a fascination for botanists. In the margin of his copy of Gerard's *Herball*, the seventeenth-century Welsh botanist Sir John Salusbury noted: '... Herbe Paris is found near Carewis in a place called Cadnant where a faire well springeth called St Michael's Well ... in Welsh, Fynnon Mihangell, within a boult shot of that well down the spring on that side of the water as Carewis standeth ... and by reason of the rankness of the place there I found a great store of herbe paris with five leaves apiece but the yeare 1606 I found the same with six leaves.' Five-leaved herb-paris still grows in this self-same wood at Coed Maesmyan, Flintshire, nearly four centuries on.[47]

Bluebell, *Hyacinthoides non-scripta* (VN: Granfer Griggles, Cra'tae – i.e. crow's toes). The sight of sheets of bluebells 'wash wet like lakes' under opening woodland leaves is one of our great wild-flower spectacles. Botanists from further east and south, used to the sweeps of colour in Alpine meadows and Mediterranean hills, still make pilgrimages to bluebell woods if they are lucky enough to be in Britain in springtime.

It is a *British* speciality, too, not just an English one. Bluebells grow in shady habitats – and in open ones in the damper west – from the cliffs of Cape Wrath in Sutherland down to Land's End. The name 'bluebell' is now almost universal, too, despite a persistent belief (held mostly by English people) that in Scotland the species is known as the wild hyacinth and that in that country 'bluebell' refers to *Campanula rotundifolia*, the summer-flowering 'harebell' of England.

But then the accepted names have always been unstable.

Two centuries ago, for instance, there is not a sign of a Scots/English split. No less a champion of the Scottish language than Robert Burns uses wild hyacinth and bluebell synonymously. In 'The Song', a poem plainly set in springtime, he rejects the gaudier flowers of foreign fields:

> *Far dearer to me are yon humble broom bowers*
> *Where the blue-bell and the gowan* [buttercup spp.]
> *lurk lowly unseen:*
> *For there, lightly tripping amongst the wild flowers,*
> *A-listening the linnet, aft wanders my Jean.*

A few decades later, England's greatest rural poet, John Clare, was using 'blue bell' and 'harebell' for the same flower in the same poem, 'The Nightingale's Nest' (*c.* 1832).[48] Even the scientific name has veered wildly about, and in reputable British Floras has changed three times since the 1980s, from *Endymion non-scriptus* to *Scilla non-scripta* to *Hyacinthoides non-scripta* in 1991. (The traditional 'non-script' – meaning 'unlettered' – portion of the name is to distinguish the British hyacinth from the classical hyacinth, a mythical flower sprung from the blood of the dying prince Hyacinthus, on whose petals Apollo inscribed the letters AIAI – 'alas' – to express his grief.)

'Bluebell' as a name did not really come into common currency until the Romantic poets began to celebrate the flower early in the nineteenth century. And it was a later Romantic, Gerard Manley Hopkins, who caught the essence of bluebells more completely than any other writer. His words throng and ripple against each other like the flowers themselves. In his Journal for 9 May 1871, he wrote: 'In the little wood/ opposite the light/ they stood in blackish spreads or sheddings like the spots on a snake. The heads are then like thongs and solemn in grain and grape-colour. But in the clough/ through the light/ they came in falls of sky-colour washing the brows and slacks of the ground with vein-blue, thickening at the double, vertical themselves and the young grass and brake fern combed vertical, but the brake struck the upright of all this with winged transomes. It was a lovely sight. – The bluebells in your hand baffle you with their inscape, made to every sense: if you draw your fingers through them they

*Bluebells are
popularly regarded
as Britain's
'national' flower.*

are lodged and struggle/ with a shock of wet heads; the
long stalks rub and click and flatten to a fan on one
another like your fingers themselves would when you
passed the palms hard across one another, making a brittle
rub and jostle like the noise of a hurdle strained by leaning
against; then there is the faint honey smell and in the
mouth the sweet gum when you bite them …'[49]

Two years later, Hopkins returned to the flower: 'May 11
– Bluebells in Hodder wood, all hanging their heads one
way. I caught as well as I could while my companions talked
the Greek rightness of their beauty, the lovely/ what people
call/ "gracious" bidding one to another or all one way, the

level or stage or shire of colour they make hanging in the air a foot above the grass, and a notable glare the eye may abstract and sever from the blue colour/ of light beating up from so many glassy heads, which like water is good to float their deeper instress in upon the mind …'

The persistent allusions to water in Hopkins's descriptions are an association that is inescapable in the field. In the Chiltern beechwoods the bluebells usually open at the same time as the beech leaves, and with the filtered light dappling the trunks and the bluebells shifting in the breeze, ambling through the flowers is like walking underwater. Even the colour of the blooms has a shoal-like quality, as they bleach from sea-blue to faded denim to spindrift grey. In my own small wood, I once mistook a steep bank of end-of-season bluebells for drifting wood-smoke. Although only 15 acres in extent, it holds individual bluebell clumps which regularly flower in colours ranging from pure white (quite common), through grey, lilac and pale blue to dark cobalt. There is also a variegated form, whose flowers have the look of a white-bell, dipped in blue water-colour paint and then allowed to run. A few hundred yards away, in a feral colony in a friend's garden, there was in 1995 a freak bluebell with bracts almost three inches long.[50] (This is apparently a rare but regular sport. In J. M. Albright's handwritten notes in my copy of The Flora of Oxfordshire, he writes of May 1917: 'Found bluebell in Dean Grove, with bracts 3 inches long, tipped with blue.' Also, half a century earlier: 'May, 1857. Found bluebell at Heythrop growing through a bush with stalks over 4 feet high and 49 bells.')

Bluebells are woodland plants, but, except perhaps in East Anglia, do not need woods so much as humidity and continuity of habitat. On lowland hedge-banks and bracken-covered pastures in the uplands, drifts of bluebells may be relics of the time when woods grew on these sites. On cliffs and in ravines in the north and west, they will grow in places that have never seen a tree, let alone a wood.

'At Lowland Point on the Lizard in Cornwall, bluebells grow among rocks and boulders only feet from the surf.'[51]

Only the toxic, acid litter of conifer plantations seems able to drive them out, and even here they can slowly move back once the conifers have been removed. In the right conditions they can persist and spread seemingly indefinitely.

In the woods at Ipsden in the Oxfordshire Chilterns, the bluebells still flourish, though they do not run 'Bluebell Trains' to see them as they did at the beginning of the century.[52] But the 'Bluebell Railway', which runs through five miles of wooded countryside between Horsted Keynes and Sheffield Park in East Sussex, was saved by a local preservation society after it was axed by British Rail in 1958. And, since 1972, Beaton's Wood at Arlington in East Sussex has been opened for a month of parish celebrations: 'Many local residents have a continued yearly commitment to the Bluebell Walk. The revenue from admissions … has helped fund several major local projects, including a school swimming pool, and the construction of a new village hall, hence the bluebell motif on the wall … [it also] pays for the upkeep of the wood, which is managed partly to enhance the aesthetic qualities of the bluebells by creating long clear vistas.'[53]

A 'Bluebell service' is held annually in Withland Wood, Leicestershire, also to raise money for charity. But recently local people report finding the surrounding wood rather bereft of flowers.[54]

The picking of bluebells can spoil woods for other visitors and is a pointless exercise, given how lifeless they look in a vase. But it does little harm to the plant itself (though one Buckinghamshire contributor was told never to pick bluebells 'with the white on' – i.e. down to the base of the stalk – as the plant would die).[55] A more serious recent development is the wholesale stripping of bluebell bulbs from woods. The cause of this, ironically, has been the fashion for 'wild' gardens, and a great increase in the demand for native bluebell bulbs. With the retail value of a single bulb currently about 10p, there is a great incentive both for the illegal 'poaching' of bulbs in public or private woods and for landowners legally to sell their bluebells to commercial diggers. (Under the Wildlife and Countryside Act of 1981, it is an offence to uproot any wild plant without the landowner's permission.) The problem is most serious in East Anglia, where bluebells are least common.[56]

But the trade is not all one way. Bluebells from local stock are being planted out in school and hospital grounds and in new plantations. And, just before the opening of the A41 Berkhamsted bypass in 1994, I saw a blue-stencilled board amongst the myriad of contractors' signs and directions. It read, cryptically, BLUEBELL TOPSOIL. But that was what it was, stripped off when the road was dug and stored. The following spring, spread along the new bare embankment outside a wood, it bloomed profusely.

A final point about names, to bring the story full circle. The Botanical Society of the British Isles (whose symbol is the bluebell) has organised a survey of pubs called the Bluebell or Blue Bell.[57] There is a conspicuous concentration of these in the East Midlands, but most have blue bells, not blue flowers, painted on their signs. Some have both. In Hunworth, Norfolk, 'in what appears to be a change of dubious taste', a previous 'Bluebell' has been renamed 'The Hunny Bell' and the sign changed to a barmaid clasping the

Spanish bluebell is a stouter, more upright species, which occurs in pink as well as white and blue. It is widely naturalised from gardens, even in ancient woods.

flower. And in the village of Helpston, Northamptonshire, birthplace of the poet John Clare, the board outside the Blue Bell has a church bell on one side and a bluebell on the other. Clare, who enjoyed bluebells, bells and beer equally, would, I think, have relished the confusion.

Spanish bluebell, *H. hispanica*, is a much stouter plant, with less nodding and more bell-like flowers which emerge from all sides of the stem. The flowers occur in purple, pink and white as well as blue. Commonly grown in gardens and naturalised in hedge-banks, churchyards and woodland edges. But the most frequently naturalised varieties are the hybrids between this species and common bluebell, *H. non-scripta* × *H. hispanica*. These crop up wherever both parents are in moderately close proximity, even in ancient woods, and the crosses (which are fertile themselves) form a complete spectrum of colours and habits between the two parents.

Ramsons or **Wild garlic**, *Allium ursinum* (VN: Stink bombs, Stinking nanny, Stinking onions, Londoner's lilies). A large stand of wild garlic in full odour is, for a couple of months a year, an impressive and unmistakable landmark. Places were named from its Old English root *hrmsa*: Ramsey Island off Pembrokeshire; Ramsbottom, Lancashire; Ramsdell, Hampshire; Ramsden and Ramsey, Essex; Ramsgreave, Lancashire; Ramsholt, Suffolk; Ramshope, Northumberland; and Ramshorn, Staffordshire.[58] In the charter for a piece of land in Berkshire granted by King Edmund to Bishop Aelfric in AD 944, one of the features used to fix the boundary in the minds of the inhabitants was a 'wild garlic wood'. A thousand years later these tangy spots, sweet-and-sour, still stick in the memory. On the Isle of Man (where there is also a 'Ramsey'): 'The motorcycle TT races are associated in some people's minds with the scent of wild garlic, as many of the places where spectators stand in mid-May are liberally covered with the plant. There are stories of fans returning from a day's racing being shunned by their friends on account of their all-pervading ambience.'[59]

'Onions were rarer than gold when we were evacuated to Ayrshire in 1940, but this was no problem, as we just went up the banks of the River Afton and picked as much wild garlic as we wanted. It seemed a kindly thought to keep posting some back to our next-door neighbour still stuck among the bombs in Liverpool. She was ever so pleased, but not so the postman. There were no polythene bags in those days, so his sack reeked permanently of the stuff till we returned three years later.'[60]

'It even made the cat smell which had been walking in it.'[61]

Perhaps it is no wonder that wild garlic's popular name is persistently mispronounced as 'ransoms'. But, for one young boy, it was not the smell, but the massed ranks of dome-shaped flowers that made him mishear their garlic tag: 'Alastair, from Bristol, aged eight at the time, confidently assured me that the white wood alliums were called Daleks. Is this how names change?'[62]

Ramsons grow in similar situations to bluebells, and often with them, but seldom actually intermixed. Although they

form dense and sometimes very large colonies, they rarely share space with other species – at least until their leaves begin to rot away at the end of May. In eastern England, they haunt the damper reaches of ancient woods. Further west and north, they become more tolerant, growing in hollow lanes, on stream-banks, and in scrubby scree, until in Pembrokeshire and Cornwall they can be found even on sheltered cliff-faces. In such places, and in the cracks in limestone pavements in the Pennines, the flower-stalks and leaves can grow up to two or three feet tall as they reach for the light. But nowhere can match the show they make on the banks of wooded streams in Wales (e.g. at Crafnant – 'the valley of the ramsons'[63] – in Snowdonia), with their green and white drifts echoing the dapple of ash leaves and trunks right to the water's edge.

Despite their strong smell *en masse*, ramsons are surprisingly mild to eat. The broad leaf-blades are used in salads, stews and soups, 'as the tin miners did in our area at the turn of the century when their wages were so low'.[64]

Oliver Rackham pops the leaves in peanut butter sandwiches when he is doing woodland fieldwork.[65] And, after I introduced the Italian owner of the village pub at the Lee, Buckinghamshire, to his local colonies, he added a flurry of wild garlic improvisations to his Tuscan menu: olive oil in which ramsons leaves had been steeped, for use on sun-dried tomatoes; ramsons salads; and ramsons leaves chopped and added, instead of basil, to a cold tomato sauce for pasta.

Daffodil, *Narcissus pseudonarcissus* (VN: Daffys, Daffy-downdilly, Lent lily, Lenten lily, Easter lily, Glens). Whatever happened to the wild daffodil? It is now a rare plant across great stretches of England and Wales, a flower that people make pilgrimages to see in a 'host'. Yet in the late sixteenth century John Gerard regarded it as growing 'almost euery where through England' and 'so well knowne to all, that it needeth no description'.[66] When the Belgian botanist Charles de l'Écluse visited England in 1581 he found that 'It grows in such profusion in the meadows close to London that in that crowded quarter commonly called Cheapside in March the country women offer the blossoms in great abundance for sale, and all the taverns may be seen decked out with this flower.'[67]

Ramsons, the woodland wild garlic – unmistakable and abundant enough to figure in Old English place names.

To judge from contemporary Floras, it continued to be one of the most widespread, common (and commonly picked) spring flowers until the middle of the nineteenth century. Then, across much of central and eastern England especially, it seemed to slip into a rapid and mysterious decline. It was not picking that was responsible (wild daffodils are no more harmed by this than cultivated varieties) even though this was deplored by, among others, the Revd Keble Martin in Devon in 1939: 'In spite of the ruthless tearing up of the plants in many districts, it still flourishes and is generally distributed.'[68]

But Devon was one of the few areas where the wild daffodil did continue to flourish. By the 1930s it had already acquired what is now one of the most curiously disjointed distributions of any once-widespread species. It occurs in widely separated zones, for instance in south Devon, pockets of the Black Mountains in Wales, stretches of the Gloucestershire–Herefordshire border country, the Sussex Weald, Farndale in Yorkshire and the Lake District. Elsewhere, even in seemingly suitable places (e.g. the lanes of south-east Cornwall),[69] it occurs in small patches many miles apart. There is a slight westerly tendency in the pat-

Wild daffodils: 'taut, pert, two yellows'.

tern, and a shift in climate may be involved in its decline. But for once, the loss of old woods and meadowland can't be seriously implicated, since in favoured regions daffodils can be abundant and quite indiscriminate in their choice of habitat. In the Blackdown Hills in Somerset, for instance, I have seen them growing around the foot of road signs, at the edges of pig-sties and on newly canalised river-banks.

There is probably no single or easy explanation for the scattering of the colonies. But the history of the trade and celebrations that have surrounded the wild daffodil in recent years does give some clues as to how its status as a 'popular' flower may have influenced its fortunes.

Nowhere has it been more popular than in the area around Newent, Dymock and Ledbury on the Gloucester-shire–Herefordshire border. This was already famous as a focus for 'Lent lilies' before the First World War. The poet Lascelles Abercrombie came to live at Ryton, close by, in 1910, and celebrated the local landscape in his best-known poem, 'Ryton Firs':

> *From Marcle way,*
> *From Dymock, Kempley, Newent, Bromberrow,*
> *Redmarley, all the meadowland daffodils seem*
> *Running in golden tides to Ryton Firs ...*[70]

The region acquired the nickname of 'The Golden Trian-gle', and in the 1930s, the Great Western Railway began running 'Daffodil Specials' from London for the sake of weekend tourists who came to walk amongst the 'golden tides' and to buy bunches at farm gates. And also for the casual workers who helped local people harvest them for the city markets. John Masefield, who was born in Ledbury, wrote of these piece-workers: 'And there the pickers come, picking for the town ... Hard-faced women, weather-beaten brown.'

This was the first place I ever saw wild daffodils myself, in the late 1970s, and I can understand very well how Londoners would travel 100 miles to see the Dymock hosts. My companion on that trip, Francesca Greenoak, had not seen them before either and her field-notes of that first impression caught their lightness and vivacity perfectly: 'The flowers themselves are lovely – taut, pert, two yellows;

the yellows of the trumpet not turning green but arching right back to the papery bud-cover; the surrounding petals appear to be forward-pointing in some (perhaps the early ones?) and stretched out in a pale star in others. In fields it looks as if they are growing in bunches.'[71]

But it was not just the dazzle and daintiness of the flowers themselves; it was their extraordinary, almost impertinent profusion. They ramped in ditches, across orchards, around the edges of arable fields, up the banks of underground reservoirs, along the Ross Spur of the M50, in amongst the bracken in young conifer plantations, and in dazzling clumps (neatly mown around) in churchyards. At the old church in Kempley, the vicar told us a little of the important role the daffodils had played in the local economy. Many farmers and orchard-owners used to regard them as a catch-crop, harvested on a 'pick-and-pay' basis. At the end of April the meadows went back to their normal business of growing hay, or fruit. But the extra income must have helped preserve many from premature 'improvement' and, our informant suspected, led to daffodil bulbs being transplanted onto holdings where they were not so common.

A 1930s guide to the village of Preston (two miles north of Dymock) fills in more detail about the spring harvest: 'They are picked by the local women and children and sold to an agent, who sends them to South Wales, where they find a ready sale for Mothering Sunday and also for Palm Sunday, for in many places the old [Welsh] custom of "flowering the graves" on that day still persists. The wild daffodils are also sent to northern industrial towns, where they find a ready sale too as they can be sold so much more cheaply than the cultivated daffodil. Some of the local boys also augment their supplies of pocket-money considerably by selling huge bunches of these flowers to passers-by at Preston Cross, where there is a continual stream of traffic to Birmingham and the Midlands and to South Wales.'

The 'Daffodil Line' to Dymock was closed in 1959 and the local daffodils faded into obscurity for a while. But in the 1980s, a new kind of daffodil consciousness began to emerge in the district, based not on picking, but on the distinctive flavour the flowers give to the local landscape: 'Many people, both local and from further afield, come to see the daffodils, and "Daffodil Teas" are held in various parish halls, e.g. Oxenhall and Kempley, to coincide with this. The flowering time is notoriously difficult to judge! ... The wild daffodil is a significant local emblem and appears in all sorts of places. It used to be on the Newent CND group banner. One of the bakeries in Newent is called The Daffodil. There is a wrought-iron gate in Newent with a row of daffodils forming part of the design.'[72]

In 1988 a 10-mile-long 'Daffodil Way' was opened between the villages of Dymock, Kempley and Four Oaks. It was created on the initiative of the Windcross Public Paths Project, with support from national and local authorities, and the co-operation of local people and farmers. It follows a roughly circular route along existing rights of way, and passes through orchards, woods, meadows and alongside lanes and streams, and is rarely without both close-up and long-distance vistas of hosts of Lent lilies.

It is clear from the survival of daffodils around Dymock and elsewhere that even commercial picking had little effect on their populations (cf. primroses, p. 72). The harvest was a consequence of local abundance, not an erosion of it, and throughout Britain, the areas in which there was extensive picking in recent memory still have the greatest concentrations of flowers. In Cornwall, Devon, Gloucestershire, Herefordshire, Hampshire and North Yorkshire they were also one of the seasonal crops of gipsies, up until the mid-1980s:

'From the woods at Tehidy, gipsies used to gather daffs to sell in Camborne, outside Woolworths on a Saturday morning.' (Cornwall)[73]

'In the 1970s the gipsies used to turn up with large baskets to pick them and take them to towns to sell.' (Hampshire)[74]

'Up to 1985 gipsies still sold the wild daffodils from door to door. I had one call at my door in Minchinhampton, Glos, a long way from Newent.'[75]

'When I was a child living at Redcar, I remember women coming round the houses selling bunches of wild daffodils from Farndale, at one old penny a bunch.' (Yorkshire)[76]

Some of these well-known local picking grounds are named after the plant: 'Wild daffodils are in and around Plymouth. Across the Tamar to the west of the city is situated

Wild daffodils, growing in almost dwarf form on the stony banks of Ullswater.

the Cornish village of Cawsand. A large population of daffs
has attracted local people for many years. It is called
"Goldie Bank".'[77]

The prefix 'Gold' also occurs, perhaps coincidentally, in
the names of a number of daffodil sites in Hertfordshire
(Golden Parsonage, Goldingtons, etc), and in the same
county there is also a well-endowed 'Dilly Wood' at
Sacombe.[78] Other woods are known locally as 'Daffy Copses'
– e.g. at Washford, near Somerset[79] – but this nickname is
almost always informal, even personal:

'During the war a small airfield was located here [Bland-
ford St Mary, Dorset], known as the Tarrant Rushton Airfield. Nissen huts were put up in the Daffy Coppice and the
servicemen lived in them for several years ... About 10 years
ago the land was returned to the owners. We were alarmed
when we saw that the hazel wood was being cleared out and
the ground ploughed up to plant some kind of fir trees.
Each spring we would visit the Daffy Coppice, and for several years the flowers were very scant. They have increased
in the last few years, and I am thrilled to tell you that this
year [1992] it is a host of golden daffodils, or as I've always
known them, Lent Lilies.'[80]

'There is a small, open wood close to where I live, about
three miles north of Chelmsford in Essex, with wild daffodils. It looks as if it was once a coppiced wood but now
has only standards. Individual wild daffodil plants are
widely separate, but occur throughout. The name "Daffy
Wood" attracted my attention and I must admit that at first
I doubted any connection with wild daffodils until I went
there and saw them for myself ... I am studying the history
of this village [Broomfield, Essex] and recently came across
a reference to the wood in a deed dated 1658. Then, it was
called "Daffadille Groves", so it appears to be a genuine
wild daffodil wood.'[81]

After Dymock and Devon, the Weald – especially in Sussex – probably provides the most extensive wild daffodil
territory, though here the flowers are more restricted to
ancient, undisturbed habitats and every individual patch
seems to be known. Well-loved colonies can be found, for
instance, in Kent at Lesnes Abbey Wood (one of the nearest
colonies of authentically wild flowers to London) and
Elchin Wood near Elmsted; in East Sussex around Ash-

down Forest and at Heathfield, Uckfield, Mayfield and Staplecross; in West Sussex, in pockets in St Leonard's Forest and on lane-banks between Horsham and Dial Post, at Fittleworth and Plaistow. Further south at Thakeham it grows in the tall, double hedges known locally as 'shaws' and in woods near Frenchlands, Steyning, where (shades of Dymock) 'my mother used to dig up clumps of the bulbs and plant them in other surrounding woods, where they have now spread'.[82]

There are local celebrations and walks in other areas. Butley Woods in Suffolk are opened to the public at daffodil time[83] (and contain a small colony of a fully double sport of *N. pseudonarcissus*, quite different from garden doubles).[84] At Dunsford, in Devon, there is a famous two-mile walk along the River Teign, where daffodils grow in profusion on the bankside and in the woods and meadows. And there are still a fair number in Gowbarrow Park, on the shores of Ullswater ('Beside the lake, beneath the trees'), whose ancestors inspired what is probably the best-known line in English poetry, Wordsworth's 'I wandered lonely as a cloud …' But for the real flavour of these doughty spring messengers in the wet and wind-swept English Lakes, read William's sister Dorothy's diary record of 15 April 1802, the 'threatening, misty morning' when they first glimpsed the host:

'When we were in the wood beyond Gowbarrow Park we saw a few daffodils close to the water-side. We fancied that the lake had floated the seeds ashore, and that the little colony had so sprung up. But as we went along there were more and yet more; and at last, under the boughs of the trees, we saw that there was a long belt of them along the shore, about the breadth of a country turnpike road. I never saw daffodils so beautiful. They grew among the mossy stones about and about them; some rested their heads upon these stones as on a pillow for weariness; and the rest tossed and reeled and danced, and seemed as if they verily laughed with the wind, that blew upon them over the lake; they looked so gay, ever glancing, ever changing. This wind blew directly over the lake to them. There was here and there a little knot, and a few stragglers higher up; but they were so few as not to disturb the simplicity, unity and life of that one busy highway.'[85]

Tenby daffodil, *N. pseudonarcissus* ssp. *obvallaris*. Some kind of daffodil is, of course, the national flower of Wales and St David. But its precise identity is uncertain. It may be the wild Lent lily. It may simply be a notional daffodil (cf. the Scotch thistle). It may even be a leek by another name, which would neatly resolve the apparent anomaly of a country having two floral symbols: 'The distinction between the daffodil and the leek is much smaller in Welsh than in English, and may be the source of the confusion as to which is the national plant: leek = Cennin; daffodil = Cennin aur (golden leek). [A botanically satisfying explanation, too, since both are lilies.]'[86]

More recently, attempts have been made to pin the honour on the Tenby daffodil. This is certainly a distinctive variety, with short, stiff stems and small, beautifully proportioned, uniformly yellow flowers in which the petals are held almost at right angles to the trumpet. It also appears to be unique to South Wales. But it was not discovered until the end of the eighteenth century, and its status as a species is still uncertain. Nevertheless it has had a fascinating history in the two centuries since, which has been reviewed by David Jones for the Tenby Museum.[87]

It was first reported by the Welsh botanist R. A. Salisbury in 1796, when it was apparently abundant in fields and pastures between Tenby and the Preseli Hills in Pembrokeshire. As it became better known, it became highly fashionable amongst horticulturalists, much to the delight of some Tenby farmers. In 1893, the curator of the Tenby Museum reported: 'From enquiries, I gather that up to 1885, a steady trade had been done by people here in the bulbs, men being sent into the country districts by one man here systematically to hunt for them. On some fields belonging to Holloway Farm, which you no doubt remember is just outside Tenby on the Marsh Road, the daffodil grew very abundantly; the owner, a man named Rees, learning of the value of the flowers at Covent Garden, sold the bulbs, the entire crop on fields, for £80.'[88]

There was also a steady trade in colourful and improbable historical myths about the flower's origins, which doubtless helped to raise its curiosity value – and price – among dealers. The bulbs had been traded by Phoenician sailors for a cargo of anthracite. They had been brought

May this glad season bring thee lasting joys!

over by Flemish settlers in the early twelfth century, or to the physic gardens of French or Italian monks, perhaps in the monastery on Caldy Island, just off Tenby. Unfortunately for all these theories of exotic introduction, nothing resembling the Tenby daffodil grows wild anywhere else in Europe.

But they helped raise the profile of the plant, and the profits of its most ruthless plunderer, Mr Shaw. According to a paper read to the Cardiff Naturalists' Society by Charles Tanfield Vachell in 1894, this ambitious nurseryman was responsible both for popularising the name 'Tenby Daffodil' and for driving the plant virtually into extinction in the wild:

'So delighted were the wholesale bulb dealers with the new flower that orders for the bulbs arrived in rapid succession. Mr Shaw was enabled to engage a staff of collectors who scoured the greater part of South Pembrokeshire for several seasons in a vigorous attempt to meet the phenomenal demand.

Considerable quantities were found by the south side of the Haven, even as far as Castlemartin, but by far the largest quantities were obtained around Narberth, Clynderwen, Llanycefn and Maenclochog.

As a rule the farmers on whose land they grew regarded them as little better than weeds and readily parted with them for a trifle and sometimes for nothing, though Mr Shaw's men, as a result of three days' excursion, often brought him a heaped cart load, which he sold for £160 or more. So well did he keep his secret that he had a complete monopoly of the trade until the supply was practically exhausted.'[89]

The ploughing of grassland during the two wars, and the intensive agriculture since, destroyed most of the colonies of putatively wild Tenby daffodils that the nineteenth-century exploitation failed to uproot. But the flower has been extensively grown in gardens around Tenby, in neighbouring Carmarthenshire and in the Aeron Valley, Cardiganshire, and is now widely naturalised in hedgebanks, churchyards and closes near to farms and cottages.[90] And in the early 1970s, a bizarre sequence of events meant that it began to spread even wider. A young boy from Essex, on holiday in the town, walked into the local tourist office and asked where he could get some Tenby daffodil bulbs to take home to his aunt. Neither Tenby's director of tourism, J. E. Evans, nor any of his staff, had ever heard of the flower and thought it was either a mistake or a practical joke. But a plumber who was working in the office heard the discussion and brought in *The Reader's Digest Book of British Flowers*, which showed and described the flower quite clearly. Mr Evans, realising the daffodil's potential prestige value, persuaded a local nurseryman to search out cultivated stocks from specialist suppliers, and featured it in the forthcoming 'Tenby in Bloom' celebrations.

Interest in the flower built up, and large quantities were planted out in the town itself. A few years later, the Tenby daffodil was given the Royal imprimatur when the Prince of Wales wore one in his buttonhole on a visit to the Principality. And in 1992, 10,000 bulbs were planted out as one of the key features of the first National Garden Festival, held at the site of a former steelworks in Ebbw Vale.

The area around Tenby is now awash with Tenby daffodils, on the verges of approach roads, on roundabouts and increasingly in gardens. Perhaps it has simply gone back to its roots, as its most likely origin centuries ago was as a spontaneous and hardy hybrid between the Lent lily and an unknown cultivar. But in remote corners of the Preseli Hills there are still a few defiantly wild clumps, floral guerrillas whose identity cannot be so tidily explained away.

But increasing numbers of daffodil cultivars are becoming naturalised as a result of widespread municipal plantings like those around Tenby, especially 'Primrose-peerless', 'Nonesuch' and varieties of Pheasant's-eye, *N. poeticus*. Ironically it was in Wales that worries about saturating country towns with cultivated daffodils were first expressed at an official level. In 1992, the Welsh Office told Abergavenny Council that it was becoming over-narcissistic and that 'there were too many daffodils in Wales'.

One much more local naturalisation has an intriguing story behind it. Amongst the fritillaries and green-winged orchids of the ancient hay meadow at Rookery Farm, Monewden in Suffolk there is a colony of the van Sion daffodil, a double-flowered, single-coloured variety first bred by a Flemish gardener in 1620. It is exceptional for garden plants to penetrate the tight sward of wild species that develops in old, undisturbed grassland and just how the van Sion effected its entry had been something of a mystery. But in 1973, John Trist tracked the plant back, along the paths and hedge-banks where it also grows, to Monewden churchyard, one mile away. There he found the daffodil growing on three graves (dated between 1830 and 1857) all belonging to members of the Garnham family, who owned Rookery Farm for generations prior to 1899. So the van Sion's source is plain enough. And perhaps it found its own way from churchyard to meadow along the footpaths and field edges. It was clearly a favourite of the Garnhams, a kind of family emblem, and they may have fancied seeing it not just as a grave ornament but in the setting of one of their working meadows.[91]

Early-purple orchid, *Orchis mascula* (VN: Adder's meat, Blue butchers, Bloody butchers, Red butchers; Goosey ganders, Kecklegs, Kettle cases, Kite's legs). The variety of local names (Grigson lists more than 90)[92] suggests that the early-purple orchid was once both abundant and well known. As late as 1950, Jocelyn Brooke described it as 'one of the few orchids that can fairly be called common in this country'.[93] It could hardly be called that now, although it is still widespread throughout Britain, occurring on most non-acidic soils, and in a great variety of habitats: ancient woodland (especially coppice), hay meadows, chalk down-land, old banks, cliff-top grassland, limestone pavements. Although it still occurs in some numbers in such places, they are precisely the kind of habitats that have suffered most from development and modern farming over the past 50 years, and where they have gone the orchid has usually vanished with them.

The early-purple orchid is a handsome plant, with spikes of pink to purple (or very occasionally white) flowers, and bold, blade-shaped leaves. The flowers usually appear at the same time as the bluebells (and often in their company), and have a distinctive, fugitive scent:

'Early-purple orchids smell wonderful when first opened, like lily of the valley, but this is soon tinged with blackcurrant. When they go over they reek of tom cat.'[94]

'This was one non-poisonous plant we never picked, and this was because locally it was called Adders' Meat. We were told by grown-ups that adders lived nearby and fed on them. As they were not plentiful perhaps this was a cunning way of preserving them, but I think the real reason was far less sophisticated, and was in fact a practical warning because the colouring of the splotched leaves bears some resemblance to a coiled adder.'[95]

Orchis means testicle, and beneath an early-purple orchid is a pair of root-tubers – one new and expanding, filling up for next year's growth, and one withering, as it supplies the plant this season. (John Ruskin was shocked when he learned the derivation of the word, and suggested that orchids be renamed 'wreatheworts'.)[96] The symbolism of the tubers' form could hardly be ignored, and some old vernacular names, such as 'dog-stones', make explicit reference to it. Concoctions of orchid root were given as aphrodisiacs back into classical times. Robert Turner, in *Botanologia* (1664), wrote that enough early-purple orchids grew in Cobham Park, Kent, to pleasure all the seamen's wives in Rochester. And they are almost certainly the 'long purples' of Shakespeare's ambiguous description of Ophelia's garland in *Hamlet*.

An unusual use for the tubers was in a drink called Saloop, or Salep. This was popular amongst manual workers in the nineteenth century, and was made by grinding the dried tubers into a flour, and mixing with hot milk or water, honey and spices. It probably originated (along, perhaps, with bulk supplies of the tubers) in the Middle East, where a similar drink is called *sahleb*.

Primroses: First Flowers

The primroses – especially the cowslip and the primrose itself – are among the best-known and most-loved of all spring flowers. The family name comes chiefly from medieval Latin and means simply the 'first rose' of the year, but it is also perhaps from the Italian *'primerole'*, 'flower of the prime' or 'firstling'. Up until the late sixteenth century it was used indiscriminately for all

members of the family. John Donne (1572–1631) wrote the earliest poem to the primrose itself:

> Upon this primrose hill,
>   Where, if Heav'n would distill
> A shower of raine, each severall drop might goe
> To his owne primrose, and grow Manna so.
>
>   ('The Primrose')

Oxlips in their heartland on the East Anglian boulder clay. Bradfield Woods, Suffolk.

Primrose, *Primula vulgaris* (VN: Spinkie). The primrose is the *prima rosa*, first flower of the year. Despite blooming almost throughout the year in sheltered Cornish hedge-banks and Sussex copses, its pure yellow flowers and tufted habit – arranged naturally into the form of a posy – have made it a universal token of spring, and especially of Easter. For generations bunches were picked as presents for parents and decoration for churches. They are also still used occasionally in the making of 'Pace' or 'Pasche' eggs: 'On Good Friday we wrapped ivy leaves, onion peelings, primrose and celandine and gorse flowers around an egg, then newspaper and string, before hard-boiling a panful of eggs to go Pasche egging on Easter Monday, with bread and butter and a packet of crisps for a picnic.'[1]

'In Chesterton Wood, Warwickshire, old Mr Tulley, who owned the wood, always opened it on Good Friday, so that local people could go and pick primroses to decorate the Churches, and his son has continued the tradition.'[2]

A woman who went to boarding school in Sussex remembers her annual Easter Botany Walk: 'We went in crocodile to Ditchling Beacon, and then broke ranks and foraged in coppiced woodland thick with primroses, which we were allowed to pick and bunch up with wool ties and send to our parents for Easter.'[3]

'Bunches were tied with wool, and then attached to a twig, which was carried horizontally, so that the flowers were not crushed.'[4]

'We used to pick very large amounts of primroses every springtime. Our lady at the Big House used to take them up to a London hospital. My mother packed the primroses in forest moss, having made the flowers into neat bunches.'[5]

'A 90-year-old friend of mine, whose family were land and mill owners in the Minchinhampton area of Gloucestershire for centuries, remembers her mother's spring wedding, when wild primroses and cowslips were strewn all along the church path for the bride to walk on.'[6]

'Primroses were an annual cash crop for the family when I was young, and my mother, sister and I daily walked miles to pick them in season. The laden baskets would be gently emptied onto the kitchen table, and we would sit for hours making up small bunches of flowers, with two leaves per bunch, tied with cotton from a sewing reel, stems trimmed

Primroses and other 'first flowers' of the spring.

to uniform length, and then placed in large, shallow bowls of water overnight. In the morning they would be carefully wrapped in tissue paper, inside cardboard flower boxes, and then one member of the family had the two-mile precariously stacked bicycle-push to Gwinear Road station, from where the boxes would steam their way to the London and Birmingham markets … Oh, to see again such abundance of primroses growing everywhere.'[7]

A more formal celebration is Primrose Day on 19 April, when primrose flowers are placed on Disraeli's statue in front of Westminster Abbey (and also on his grave at Hughenden in Buckinghamshire).[8] They were the politician's favourite flower, and Queen Victoria regularly sent him bunches from Windsor and Osborne. After his death in 1881, the botanist Sir George Birdwood suggested inaugurating a 'Primrose Day' and the custom has been kept up ever since.

The picking of primroses, especially *en masse* ('Gipsies used to pick pillowcases full to sell in Devon towns in 1930s and 40s'),[9] began to get a bad name in the more conservation-minded 1970s and 80s. Yet there has never been any real evidence that picking primroses, as distinct from digging them up by the root, has any effect on their numbers. Oliver Rackham can find no correlation between public access and primrose abundance in East Anglia, and puts three of the most publicly used rural woods in the region amongst his top twenty primrose woods.[10] And in Devon, a local and little-known commercial enterprise, involving extensive primrose-picking, led to an investigation which for the most part confirmed that little harm resulted.

In the early part of this century, the owner of Hele papermill in South Devon decided to bring 'a breath of Devon air' to the buyers of his paper. He arranged for bunches of primroses to be picked and sent off to valued customers. The primroses were picked from woods and hedgerows by the wives and children of the mill-workers. 'Local boys and girls picked the primroses in March and April – 25 primroses and 5 leaves in each bunch tied with string, and took them to the Mill, where they were boxed up and sent. My son and daughter partook of this "pocket-money" exercise which had gone on for years before we moved here.'[11]

The custom soon spread to other Devon paper-mills and

continued when most of the smaller firms were bought up by the Wiggins Teape Group. But in the mid-1970s, the company received a good deal of adverse publicity about what they were doing, and in 1977 they invited a team of ecologists from Plymouth Polytechnic to make an independent assessment of the effects of the annual harvest.

Although the team uncovered a certain amount of *ad hoc* picking by children, most was done on a contract basis on a few farms in the South Hams district. The numbers picked seem, on the surface, to have been prodigious. In 1978, some 13,000 boxes of primroses, containing a total of 1,300,000 blooms, were mailed out. But the operation was carefully organised, with no evidence of mass picking. 'Only a few blooms were picked from any one plant at any one time; for the packaging and posting process, only immature blooms can be used, so that the recipient receives fresh lasting material (which can last from seven to 14 days). Thus the pickers selected young blooms, and open flowers remained on the plants. Clearly, although the picking reduces the total number of flowers able to set seed, no plant has all of its flowers removed.' The Plymouth team also noted that 'all involved in the operation, farmers, pickers, packers and organisers at the hall, enjoyed being involved, and the annual event, lasting for up to three weeks, was regarded as something of an occasion.' [12]

A number of comparative plots were set up, and the team's preliminary conclusion was that 'the level of picking carried out is not a serious biological threat to the survival of *Primula vulgaris* in the South Hams', especially as individual plants seemed to have a life of about 15 to 25 years.

But the custom was wound up a few years later, in the light of hardening public attitudes towards wild-flower picking and a perceived reduction in primrose populations nationwide. Whether this had anything to do with picking is doubtful. Primroses have always had a rather odd and scattered distribution, both locally and nationally. Where they have declined or disappeared, it is usually as a result of their habitat becoming unsuitable – drained, sprayed, or shaded out perhaps. Where they do not occur, it is usually because the local climate or soil does not suit them.

In 1944, Professor Ronald Good published a classic study of the distribution of primroses in Dorset. He trav-

elled 'every road and major track in Dorset' and discovered
a distinct pattern as to where primroses did, and did not,
grow. In the west they occurred in woods and hedge-banks.
In the east they were largely confined to woods. Nowhere
did they grow in hedge-banks but *not* in adjacent woods;
and there were two conspicuous areas in which there were
virtually no primroses at all. Professor Good explained the
pattern in terms of the distribution of soils and rainfall in
the county. Primroses seem to prefer damp conditions, and
the rainfall is noticeably higher in the west. Although
hedge-banks dry out more quickly than woods, in the west
they are always moist enough to support primroses. In the
east only woods on clays and loams are usually sufficiently
moist. The two primrose 'gaps' corresponded roughly with
the chalk and sand areas, which have poor water-holding
capacity.[13]

It is an explanation which at first sight seems to hold true
for the country as a whole. In the extreme west, primroses
will grow anywhere – on sea-cliffs, stone walls, even along
the middle of country roads. The further east you move,
especially into chalky areas, the more they are confined to
woods and shady banks. But problems arise when you consider an area such as central Suffolk, where the rainfall is on
average less than half that of east Dorset but where primroses still grow abundantly in many hedge-banks. Some of
these are ancient sites, perhaps once the bank-and-ditch system of ancient woods, so perhaps continuity plays a part.
But so, clearly, does disturbance. Primroses have not only
colonised new motorway banks on unsuitably dry soils, but
have shown a great willingness to spread where paths are
opened up or broadened in woods. This is partly because of
the increased light. But trampling and traffic help shift the
primroses' rather immobile seeds that otherwise have to
rely on rain-splash or the packhorse labours of ants to move
even short distances.

Oliver Rackham has suggested other factors in the equa-
tion and believes that primroses will really prosper only
where soils are rich and have a higher than average level of
mineral nutrients. And, though they can tolerate deep
shade, they need regular bursts of light to flower and set
seed. In Buff Wood, Cambridgeshire, an area of coppice was
cut for the first time in over 60 years. The primroses, which

Ian Hickling's plan of his wild Primula corner, with pressed specimens of each variety and a map of their spatial relations (see p. 79).

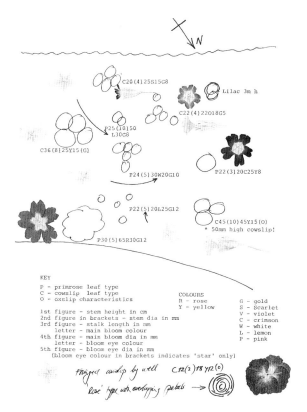

C20(4)25S15G8

Lilac 3m h

C22(4)22O18G5

P25(10)50
L30G8

C36(8)25Y15(G)

P24(5)30W20G10

P22(3)20C25Y8

P22(5)20L25G12

C45(10)45Y15(O)
* 50mm high cowslip!

P30(5)65R30G12

KEY
P - primrose leaf type
C - cowslip leaf type
O - oxslip characteristics   COLOURS
                                              R - rose   G - gold
1st figure - stem height in cm   Y - yellow   S - Scarlet
2nd figure in brackets - stem dia in mm   V - violet
3rd figure - stalk length in mm   C - crimson
           letter - main bloom colour   W - white
4th figure - main bloom dia in mm   L - lemon
           letter - bloom eye colour   P - pink
5th figure - bloom eye dia in mm
           (bloom eye colour in brackets indicates 'star' only)

Fringed cowslip by wall   C12(2)18 Y12(0)
'Rose' type with overlapping petals →

had been inconspicuous, began to flower in the following November and produced at least a hundred times their usual output of flowers for the next eighteen months.[14]

In any of these large populations, and especially in the great linear colonies along West Country hedge-banks, you will notice variations in the colour, texture and size of primrose flowers. Any with pure white flowers may be escaped specimens of one of the Mediterranean subspecies (sspp. *balearica* and *sibthorpii*).[15] But the native species can produce flowers in every shade from deep yellow to palest cream, including a delightful variety with white flowers round a pale yellow 'eye'. There is also a pink – or more accurately rhubarb-and-custard – form. It is most frequent in churchyards and on banks close to villages, so there is some doubt about its origins. But it also occurs in much wilder sites, especially in west Wales, and is so constant in its coloration that it is almost certainly a genetically different native form: 'Pink primroses grow in a little wooded hollow, near a small pool on a steep bank, close to the water and shaded by trees, and also alongside a small stream flowing into the pool. They have grown in this location for many years. The site is at least ¼ mile from the nearest house, and there is no path or track near to it.' [16]

As well as colour varieties, primrose flowers can adopt unusual, even bizarre forms. The commonest is the umbellate form (var. *caulescens*), in which the flowers form a spray on top of a longer, cowslip-like stalk. Doubles also occasionally spring up as chance sports, and one with soft shell-pink flowers has recently been taken into commercial cultivation as 'Sue Jervis'. Much rarer, though greatly prized by early cottage gardeners, are Jack-in-the-greens, where the normal calyx is replaced by a ruff of miniature primrose leaves, and hose-in-hose, in which a second complete flower grows through the centre of the first. And Gerard described an extraordinary 'amiable and pleasant kind' found in a wood at Clapdale near Settle: 'it bringeth forth among the leaues a naked stalke of a grayish or ouerworne greenish colour: at the top whereof doth growe in the winter time one flower and no more, like vnto that single one of the fielde; but in the sommer time it bringeth foorth a soft russet huske or hose, wherin are conteined many smal flowers, sometimes fower or fiue, and oftentimes more, very thicke thrust together, which maketh one entire flower, seeming to be one of the common double Primroses, whereas indeed it is one double flower made of a number of smal single flowers, neuer ceassing to beare flowers winter nor sommer, as before is specified.' [17] (I have seen something similar in 'fasciated' primulas, where the stalks of several flowers fuse together. In one garden in Wigginton, Hertfordshire, a specimen appeared in which the stems had virtually disappeared. It was like an alpine primrose, with the flowers forming a tight, tufted dome amidst a wreath of leaves.)

There are, finally, less festive strains amongst the primrose's cultural associations. Shakespeare's metaphor of the 'primrose path of dalliance' in *Hamlet* is a long way from the Victorian custom of planting primroses on the graves of small children. In parts of Buckinghamshire these are often on the west side of the churchyard, producing sadder paths of primrose yellow in April. [18]

Oxlip, *P. elatior* (VN: Paigle). The 'oxlip' which Shakespeare features on his 'bank where the wild thyme blows' and again, in *The Winter's Tale*, where Perdita distinguishes it by the adjective 'bold', is not *Primula elatior*, but what is now more usually known as the false oxlip, a hybrid between the primrose and the cowslip (see below). The true oxlip had not even been officially discovered when Shakespeare was writing and was presumably taken, by ordinary country people and botanists alike, for one of those aberrant forms that primroses are apt to throw up. Its blooms are a similar shape and colour to primrose's, but smaller and more bell-like, and are held in a graceful, drooping, one-sided cluster at the top of the stalk.

The true oxlip has drooping, bell-shaped pale yellow flowers held chiefly on one side of the stem.

Yet, despite the fact that they have a very limited distribution in eastern England, oxlips must have grown in some woods, as now, in colonies millions strong; and the comparative lateness of their recognition is nearly as puzzling as that of the fritillary (see p. 31). John Ray made the first definite record of 'Primula veris elatior pallido flore' in 'Kingston and Madingley woods [Cambridgeshire] abundantly and elsewhere' in 1660.[19] But the standard botanical work of the late eighteenth and early nineteenth centuries, Sowerby's *English Botany*, though carrying a picture of the true oxlip, rejects it as a separate species: 'In describing the Primrose, we expressed a suspicion that the Oxlip might be a variety of that rather than the Cowslip, or possibly a hybrid between the two. We are still much inclined to the latter opinion and that it has originated from a Primrose impregnated by a Cowslip; its external habit, the contraction towards the middle of the leaf, and the umbellate flower-stalk indicating (according to Linnaeus's ingenious idea) the father, while the blossom itself, in form, colour and scent, most resembles its mother.'[20]

It was not until the 1840s that two Essex botanists, George Gibson and Henry Doubleday, finally clinched the matter. It was Doubleday's observations of the plants around the village of Great Bardfield in Essex that was crucial: 'They cannot be hybrids, for the primrose does not exist in the parish and these oxlips grow by the thousand in the meadow and in the moist woody places adjoining: in one instance a meadow of about two acres is entirely covered by them, being a mass of yellow bloom.'[21]

The species was subsequently named 'the Bardfield Oxlip' to distinguish it from the primrose–cowslip hybrid. Alas, it no longer grows in Great Bardfield, or in many of its previous haunts (including old meadowland – of which there is precious little left in East Anglia). But it has survived in a triangle of land on the boulder clay between Stansted in Essex and Bury St Edmunds and Stowmarket, Suffolk, and in a smaller area west of Cambridge. In these areas it grows in most of the ancient woods, sometimes in great quantities and occasionally replacing the primrose altogether. It is even hanging on in some non-woodland habitats, such as damp field-edges and hedgerows. A hedge-bank near Dovedenhall Wood, Suffolk, is typical in being a relic of a wing of the wood which was grubbed out around 1800.

The few oxlip 'outliers' may be relics on a much grander scale, isolated remnants of a time when oxlips were more widespread in southern and eastern England. One is at Dickleburgh Fen in Norfolk. Another is between Berkhamsted and Bovingdon, on the Hertfordshire–Buckinghamshire border, in a group of four woods on a chalk–clay soil not unlike boulder clay. They came to light in the early 1970s, and there is a slight possibility that they were planted by a local clergyman, the Revd Moule, who was noted for such botanical evangelism. But if so he was very thorough, as some of the colonies are in remote, barely visited spots. It is more feasible that they are a genuinely wild, relict population, especially as the four woods were once part of a large, continuous stretch of ancient woodland.[22]

All the oxlip populations are probably in a roughly stable state at present. Like primroses, they have benefited greatly where coppicing has been reintroduced. But this has been offset by the increased number of deer and pheasants in East Anglia, which have a taste for the blossoms. Oxlips hybridise with both the cowslip and primrose, producing an almost complete range of intermediate types. There are even occasional pink oxlips, though these are usually the result of crosses with garden primulas. In his garden in Berkshire, Ian Hickling found an oxlip hybrid with the characteristic one-sided bell-flower habit, but bearing blooms of a 'vivid red-terracotta' with oxlip-yellow 'eyes': 'This plant is a natural seedling from the many primulas I have growing here, and a descendant of an oxlip plant brought from East Anglia in 1963, planted in Moulton, Northamptonshire, and then brought here in 1973, from which hybrids with primrose and cowslip have appeared.'[23]

Given the attractiveness of the oxlip's habit, it is surprising that such little use of it has been made in breeding garden primulas.

Cowslip, *P. veris* (VN: Hey-flower, Peggles, Paigles). Cowslip wine, cowslip balls ('tisty-tosties'), cowslips strewn on bridal paths and worn as chaplets on May Day – the cowslip's cultural history suggests a flower that was once as abundant and accessible as the buttercup. No wonder that its dramatic decline between the 1950s and 1980s was felt so keenly in the countryside.

'One bank holiday the family went to Chingford Plain for the day. There were a dense mass of holidaymakers like ourselves escaping the dirt and grime of our home streets in East London. We found a solitary cowslip where no doubt all its companions had been picked. We encamped and my grandmother sat by the flower all day with it covered by a paper bag to prevent anyone else noticing it. We left that evening with that one flower still intact hoping it would survive at least until the next weekend.'[24]

As with the primrose, it was not over-picking that put paid to cowslips in so many parishes, but the relentless advance of modern farming, especially the ploughing of old grassland and a massive extension in the use of chemical herbicides (which extended to wayside management up to the mid-1980s). And banished along with the flower went a host of vernacular names, for instance 'culverkeys' and 'bunch of keys', from the jiggling egg-yolk flowers that John Clare delightfully called 'cowslip-peeps'; 'freckled face', from the orange spots that lie at the base of the petals, and which Shakespeare thought were the source of the flower's faintly fruity, dill-like scent. (In *A Midsummer Night's Dream*, the fairy chants: 'In their gold coats spots you see/ Those be rubies, fairy favours,/ In those freckles live their savours ...') In George Meredith's novel *The Ordeal of Richard Feverel* (1859), there is even a cowslip malapropism on a par with 'wooden enemies' for 'wood anemones': on forages with his unrequited lover, Richard used to call the flowers 'coals-sleeps'. Now we are reduced to 'paigle', which today is used rather indiscriminately for any wild primula, and 'cowslip' itself, which, though it hasn't the most pretty of origins (it is a euphemism for 'cow-slop' or cow-pat), does at least hint at the kind of company cowslips like to keep.

In Lambley, Nottinghamshire, a dearth of wild specimens has meant that the ceremony of 'Cowslip Sunday' has had to resort to garden-grown flowers: 'Cowslip Sunday is celebrated in Lambley on the first Sunday in May. Nowadays the occasion is marked by having a basket of cowslips on the altar at the morning service in the Parish Church ... Formerly, when cowslips grew more profusely in the wild, parties of people travelled out from nearby Nottingham on

Cowslips saved from the mower in a Cambridgeshire churchyard.

Cowslip Sunday to buy bunches of cowslips picked by local children. Some local residents, now in their eighties, remember selling the flowers to day trippers. There is said to have been a special Cowslip Sunday hymn but this is now forgotten.'[25]

But in the 1990s, the cowslip is showing signs of recovery. On the chalky and light-soiled areas of England and Wales that were its stronghold, it has begun to return to unsprayed verges and village greens and to colonise the banks of new roads – no doubt assisted here and there by the scattering of wild-flower seed-mixtures. On downland where grazing pressures have eased, for instance at Tring Park, Hertfordshire, vast masses have reappeared. (Cowslips seem to flower more profusely amongst rank grasses and scrub than amongst large numbers of spring-grazing sheep.) And they are flourishing in the increasing number of churchyards that are being looked after with an eye to their wildlife. Lambley may yet be able to use wild flowers again in its ancient ceremony.

Cowslips share in their family's tendency to produce a profusion of sports and variations, and churchyards are probably the most likely place to find orange-flowered forms and the variety known to gardeners as 'Devon Red'. These are hard to differentiate from conventional cowslips except by their colour and are almost certainly natural, native forms. But, as they are seen most often in mixed populations of primulas, close to habitations, there is always the possibility that some are back-crosses with red polyanthuses (themselves originally crosses between the cowslip and various primroses).[26] Another unusual form is recorded in some handwritten notes in the back of my copy of Druce's *Flora of Oxfordshire* (1886), made by a previous owner, J. M. Albright: 'May 1913. Found cowslip in Henley Nap, 15 inches high with 87 flowerets on the stem. Two other cowslips on same root about 10 or 12 inches high, had 43 and 49 flowerets respectively.'

Primula hybrids. All the above species (including their various forms) hybridise with each other. The commonest cross is between the primrose and the cowslip, which gives rise to the 'false oxlip', *P. vulgaris* × *P. veris*. This occurs wherever both species are frequent and differs from the true oxlip in holding its primrose-like flowers upright and

Plants from a hybrid swarm of Primulas in Barking churchyard, Suffolk, showing colour variants of the primrose and of the crosses between primrose and cowslip ('false oxlips' – the chief ancestor of the polyanthus).

splayed at the top of the flower-stalk. It is the chief ancestor of garden polyanthuses.

But wherever cultivated primulas and polyanthuses (especially red-flowered species and varieties such as the purple-flowered *P. juliae* from the Caucasus and *P. hirsuta* from the Alps) grow in the proximity of wild species, extraordinary progeny can result, including what are known as 'hybrid swarms', in which all kinds of intermediates and back-crosses occur. (Churchyards are famous for this kind of miscegenation, e.g. at Barking in Suffolk.)

In 1839, the floriculturalist Charles M'Intosh reported in the magazine *The Flower Garden* that a Mr Herbert had 'raised from the natural seed of one umbel of a highly manured red cowslip, a primrose, a cowslip, oxlips of the usual and other colours, a black polyanthus, a hose-in-hose cowslip and a natural primrose bearing its flowers on a polyanthus stalk. From the seed of that hose-in-hose cowslip I have since raised a hose-in-hose primrose.'

A comparable swarm arose in the wild primula corner of Ian Hickling's garden in 1994 (see above), including one particularly striking throwback: 'a cowslip hybrid which has evolved a petal fringe colour rather after the fashion of the old "gold-laced" polyanthus, despite there being no flower of that type around to my knowledge last year when hybridisation took place.'[27]

The story of how the great range of garden primulas and polyanthus was developed from these natural crosses is told at length in Roy Genders' *Collecting Antique Plants* (1971).

Lanes and Fields

The explosion of spring colour in open country, where there is no obstruction to sunlight, comes a couple of weeks later than the early May climax in woodland. True, there are earlier wayside flowers, colt's-foot and celandine, for instance; and refugees from woodland, such as primrose, violet and ramsons, bloom earlier on sunny banks and road

verges than they do in shade. But mid-May marks the simultaneous blooming of woodland flowers such as these and the species whose original home may have been the woodland glade – cow parsley, red campion, greater stitchwort, lady's-smock and germander speedwell.

Dame's-violet, a cottage garden favourite now widely naturalised.

Marsh-marigold, *Caltha palustris* (VN: Kingcup, May-flower, May-blobs, Mollyblobs, Pollyblobs, Horse-blob, Water-blobs, Water-bubbles, Gollins, the Publican). This is one of the most ancient native plants, probably surviving the glaciations and flourishing after the last retreat of the ice, in a landscape inundated by glacial meltwaters. Until two centuries ago, before the extensive draining of the land-scape, kingcups must have been the most conspicuous plant of early spring, blooming at the edges of cattle wallows, in

Marsh-marigolds provide the first show of spring colour in meadowland.

water-meadows and damp flashes on village greens, and growing straight from the dark mud amongst willow and alder roots in wet woods. In the Isle of Man, where plant rituals survived until very recently, it was held in high regard as a spring omen, and flowers were strewn on doorsteps on old May Eve. Now the custom of bringing 'mayflower' – as it is called in English on the island – into the house is enjoying something of a revival, and improvised vases of blooms have been seen on counters and in shop windows.[1]

Marsh-marigolds are in decline as agricultural land continues to be drained, but they are still the most three-dimensional of plants, their fleshy leaves and shiny petals impervious to wind and snow, and standing in sharp relief against the tousled brown of frostbitten grasses. Most of the plant's surviving local names – water-blobs, mollyblobs, water-bubbles – reflect this solidity, especially the splendid, rotund 'the publican' from Lancashire.[2]

The white forms found in gardens are a foreign variety. But Francis Simpson distinguishes a native form with lemon-yellow flowers and taller habit.[3]

Pasqueflower, *Pulsatilla vulgaris*. One of the most beautiful of our native flowers. Its purple petals, held in the shape of a bell, surround a tuft of yellow stamens, and are cushioned on greyish, feathery leafage. It blooms around Eastertime – hence the name 'Pasque', meaning, like 'Paschal', of Easter. But it has never been common enough to have much of a place in local culture. There was a legend in a few areas that it sprang from the blood of Danes or Romans, because it seemed to haunt old earthworks such as barrows and boundary banks. But this association was more likely due to the pasqueflower's need for the kind of undisturbed chalk grassland often found at antiquarian sites. Such places have always been comparatively safe from ploughing, and the pasqueflower can have a long occupation on them. Until the 1970s it grew on the Fleam Dyke in Cambridgeshire, where the East Anglian poet Edward Fitzgerald knew it in the mid-nineteenth century and commented on it in an annotation to his *Omar Khayyam*. Not many miles away, another nineteenth-century poet, John Clare, found it around the village of Helpston in Northamptonshire:

'You have often wished for a blue Anemonie the
Anemonie pulsitilis of botanists & I can now send you
some for I have found some in flower to day which is very
early but it is a very early spring the heathen mythology is
fond of indulging in the metramorphing [*sic*] of the
memory of lovers & heroes into the births of flowers
& I coud almost fancy that this blue anenonie [*sic*] sprang
from the blood or dust of the romans for it haunts the
roman bank in this neighbourhood & is found no were else
it grows on the roman bank agen swordy well & did grow
in great plenty but the plough that destroyer of wild
flowers has rooted it out of its long inherited dwelling it
grows also on the roman bank agen Burghley Park in
Barnack Lordship.'

Letter to his publisher, 25 March 1825[3]

*The pasqueflower –
the anemone of
Passiontide – is now
reduced to a scatter
of sites on old
grassland in chalk
and limestone
country.*

It continues to grow in some quantity at Barnack, in the old stone quarry known as the Hills and Holes, which is just a couple of miles down the road from Burghley Park.

Pasqueflower is now a nationally scarce plant. Its largest colony is on the steep banks of Barnsley Warren in the Cotswolds; the smallest probably the few flowers that cling on in short turf on the Magnesian limestone in West Yorkshire – its most northerly station in Britain.[5]

Lesser celandine, *Ranunculus ficaria*. This is one of the first woodland flowers of the year. More than two hundred years ago Gilbert White noted that the average first flowering around his Hampshire village of Selborne was 21 February.[6] A century later, the Hertfordshire botanist John Hopkinson gave precisely the same date for the years between 1876 and 1886. Another hundred years on, and this is still the time celandines begin to bloom across much of southern England in a typical year – justifying one of celandine's defunct local names, 'spring messenger'.

Another obsolete name is pilewort – the herb given for haemorrhoids. This ancient prescription is based on the Doctrine of Signatures, and on a fancied resemblance between the knobbly tubers and piles. These tubers – which readily break free from the fibrous roots – are one of the means by which celandines are able to spread rapidly in the open and disturbed soil of damp woodland tracks and to colonise stream-banks, ditches and shady gardens. A subspecies, ssp. *bulbilifer*, is an even more aggressive spreader. It has tiny bulblets – 'bulbils' – in the junctions between the leaf-stalks and the main stem, and these are readily strewn about by birds, walkers, car tyres and flowing water.

The most curious name is celandine itself, which derives from the Greek *chelidon*, a swallow. The sixteenth-century herbalist Henry Lyte suggested that this was because it 'beginneth to springe and to flowre at the comming of the swallows'.[7] But most celandines are in flower long before the swallows arrive, and it looks as if the lesser celandine may have been confused with the greater celandine, another yellow-flowered but quite unrelated species.

But perhaps the flower's name indicates something less literal than a coincidence between blossoming and a bird's arrival. Perhaps lesser celandine was seen as a kind of vegetable swallow, the flower that, like the bird, signalled the

Lesser celandine or 'pilewort'. The knobbly root tubers resemble piles and, according to the Doctrine of Signatures, were given as a treatment for them. Herbal plants which sprang up in the sanctified ground of the churchyard were regarded as being especially powerful.

arrival of spring. Wordsworth certainly thought so. It was his favourite flower and he wrote three poems about it. Before the first, 'To the Small Celandine', he adds a little field-note: 'It is remarkable that this flower, coming out so early in the Spring as it does, and so bright and beautiful, and in such profusion, should not have been noticed earlier in English verse. What adds much to the interest that attaches to it is its habit of shutting itself up and opening out according to the degree of light and temperature of the air.'

The second poem ('To the Same Flower') includes a stanza about children's enjoyment of the celandine's 'glittering countenance':

> *Soon as gentle breezes bring*
> *News of winter's vanishing,*
> *And the children build their bowers,*
> *Sticking 'kerchief-plots of mould*
> *All about with full-blown flowers,*
> *Thick as sheep in shepherd's fold!*
> *With the proudest Thou art there,*
> *Mantling in the tiny square.*[8]

When Wordsworth died in 1850, it was proposed that a celandine would be the most fitting decoration for his tomb in the Lakes. But, ironically, the plant carved on the monument at Grasmere seems not to be 'the Small Celandine' at all, but, because of the old confusion or inept carving, the greater, *Chelidonium majus*.

Perhaps, after celandine's long history of ambivalent medicinal and classical names, a modern, serendipitous tag, accidentally coined by a child, deserves the last word: 'When my daughter was a toddler she mispronounced celandine as "lemon-eye", and since that is what the flower looks like that is what we call it.'[9]

Greater stitchwort, *Stellaria holostea* (VN: Headaches, Stinkwort, Wedding cakes, Milkmaids, Star-of-Bethlehem, Brassy buttons, Shirt buttons, Poor-man's-buttonhole, Daddy's-shirt-buttons, Snapdragon, Poppers). This is a familiar spring flower of hedge-banks and wood-rides, much loved for its modestly beautiful white flowers, which have been likened to – and no doubt used as – buttonholes. Other local names, some of which have survived, remark on the ease with which the stalks break (snapdragons, snapcrackers) and its habit of noisily firing off its seeds (poppers, pop-guns). A woman from Kent recalled to a contributor how this became a childhood game while her family picked hops: 'When her mother and family went hop-tying in May she was pushed to the hop garden in a wooden baby cart. This was then filled round her with tangled stems of greater stitchwort from the hedgerows, with all the round seed capsules already ripening, the popping of which would keep her absorbed and occupied while her mother tied the bines.'[10]

Red campion, *Silene dioica* (VN: Adder's flower, Robin Hood, Cuckoo flower). One of a dozen or so spring flowers that share a name, and a season, with the cuckoo, red campion is at its best where it grows with bluebells and white stitchwort and ramsons, in hedgerows, in woods, and on northern and western sea-cliffs. But it has an oddly patchy distribution, abundant, sometimes, in one parish and absent from the next, even though there are no obvious habitat differences. Although the flowers are most usually rose-red, pink- and white-bloomed varieties are common. Red campion also hybridises with its close relative white campion to produce another range of intermediate-coloured flowers.

Greater stitchwort – 'poor-man's-buttonhole' – decorating a Hampshire hedge-bank in late April.

Thrift, *Armeria maritima* (VN: Sea-pink, Cliff clover, Ladies' cushions, Heugh daisy). An accommodating perennial found in almost every kind of seashore location. The compact pink-flowered cushions grow on sand-dunes, shingle, marshland edges, cliffs, even stone walls near the sea. The origin of the most commonly used name, thrift, is obscure; it may derive from 'thriving', i.e. evergreen, or, more likely I suspect, from the tight and economic tufting of the leaves, which serves as a way of conserving the plant's fresh water in salt winds. Geoffrey Grigson memorably described ambling across acres of these padded cushions on Annet in the Isles of Scilly as like 'a dream of walking on soft rubber which has squirted into flower'.[11]

At any rate, 'thrift' was once well enough known to be used as a punning emblem on the back of the old twelve-sided threepenny bit, the coin whose awkwardness made it the most frequently consigned to money-boxes. It is still the emblem of the Fourth City Building Society.

'Heugh daisy' is a very local Scots and northern name, from 'heugh', meaning a cliff or ravine.

Thrift's blooms can vary from deep pink to white, and they have been a favourite for garden edging at least as far back as the sixteenth century, when John Gerard recommended them 'for the bordering vp of beds and bankes'.[12] This, of course, is exactly how the hazy pink flowers and neat green cushions seem to arrange themselves in the wild, fringing the tops of Devon drystone walls, lining rock crevices in Pembrokeshire, or clustering around the high-tide line on Lancashire sand-dunes.

Other varieties of sea-pink, some of them quite large, occur a long way from the sea, on mountains and river shingles – relics of the post-glacial era, when the species was probably widespread in rocky open country. They also have a taste for lead-rich soils and are often found on mine-spoil tips. The thrift family's scientific name, *Plumbaginaceae*, derives from the ancient belief that they could cure lead poisoning: 'In a picnic place near Woodhall in Wensleydale [40 miles from the sea], where a stream running from the old lead-mines often floods the area, there is often a wonderful display of thrift. Some say that this is a relic of the wooden bungalows that were erected there by a philanthropist for city dwellers. But with thrift being a Plumbago, I feel it may have been there first.' [13]

Right: thrift – which may have acquired this common name from its tight and economic tufts.

Charles Rennie Mackintosh's portrait of thrift or sea-pink, painted on Holy Island, 1901.

Goat willow, *Salix caprea*, and **grey willow**, *S. cinerea* (VN: Sallow, Pussy willow). These are the commonest and most widespread willows in Britain, growing in ditches, reedbeds, scrub, wet woodland, hedges and urban waste-land. They are best known for the silky, silver-grey male catkin buds – the 'pussy willows' – which appear in late January and become brilliant yellow in March. (They used to be called 'goslings' at this stage, because their texture and colour were like newly hatched geese.) Because so little else was in leaf or flower at this early season, sprays of sallow have frequently been used as 'palm' to decorate churches

'Pussy willow', or 'goslings' – the male catkins of goat willow.

or to carry in processions at Eastertide.

'I remember attending Sunday School on Palm Sunday and wearing a sprig of pussy willow, and my father was always told "You get your hair pulled if you don't wear a piece of palm on Palm Sunday." '[14]

'As a child I used to make puppets out of pussy willows. To do this, take about 10 pussy willows, while they are still silvery, before the pollen appears, and thread them on white cotton. This takes patience and some of them will break, so you need some spares. Put knots on either end of the cotton to stop them falling off. Attach more cotton for the strings and tie these to a twig. Move the twig and the puppet wriggles like a snake.'[15]

Wallflower, *Erysimum cheiri* (VN: Gilliflower, Milkmaids). A species native only in rocky places in southern Greece and the Aegean. The wild forms have very fragrant yellow or brownish-orange flowers and it was for these that the plant was introduced to Britain at an early date. There is a story that it was often planted on the walls of castles and manor houses so that the scent could waft through the windows of the bedchambers. Whatever their origins, yellow-flowered plants indistinguishable from wild specimens have clung on to many ancient buildings and walls – for instance, Bury St Edmunds Abbey, Suffolk; Holy Island Priory, Northumberland; Waltham Abbey and the castle and Roman walls at Colchester, Essex; and many of the Oxford colleges. Plants closer to garden varieties appear more widely, on stonework in churchyards and railway cuttings, for example. Having very lightweight seeds which can be carried upwards by the wind, they sometimes take root even on chimneys.

A different species, the violet-flowered *Erysimum linifolium*, has been christened 'the Manx wallflower' on the Isle of Man and 'has been known on the ruins of Rushen Abbey and nearby quarries for more than a hundred years'.[16]

Dame's-violet, *Hesperis matronalis*, is a cottage-garden favourite introduced from Europe in the sixteenth century, and now increasingly naturalised in waste places and on roadside verges, but rarely far from houses. The flowers can range from purple to white, and have a sweet violet scent (though this is less evident in the purple varieties).

Cuckooflower or **Lady's-smock**, *Cardamine pratensis* (VN: Our Lady's smock, Milkmaids, Fairy flower, May flower, Coco plant). Cuckooflower is the 'approved' English name for this common and widespread species of damp grassland, roadsides, ditches and river-banks. But 'lady's-smock' is both more current and more expressive. The flowers vary in colour from very pale pink to mauve, and are slightly cupped or 'frocked' (though 'smock' was once less than complimentary slang for a woman, on a par with our 'bit of skirt', and there may be allusions in the name to what went on in springtime meadows).

In some places the flowers can be so dense as to colour the ground: 'In Norfolk I always knew it by its other com-

Caroline May's painting of cuckooflowers. The double variety (left) and hose-in-hose (right) were painted from specimens in the vicarage orchard at South Petherwyn, Cornwall, in 1852.

mon name of Ladies Smock and also as Milkmaids. I remember they grew in such abundance on my local common (South Wootton, just outside King's Lynn) that I could pick armfuls every day. There are pictures of me [c. 1970] with my arms full posing, ironically, beside the massive pipes which were soon to drain the common and denude it of its glorious pinky-mauve display.'[17]

In parts of Devon the double-flowered form *flore pleno*, and even hose-in-hose forms (where one normal bloom grows through the centre of another – cf. primrose, p. 76) are not uncommon.[18]

As for 'cuckooflower', it is a name which this species has shared, at a local level, with at least a dozen or so other spring flowers, including wood anemone, red campion, greater stitchwort, wood-sorrel, bluebell and early-purple orchid, and the coincidence of its flowering with the arrival of the cuckoo is probably no better than for any of these other species.[19] In fact, in the south of England it is usually in flower by March, and in the extreme south-east often as early as February after a mild winter: 'My birthday falls on 14 April, and when I was a child my father told me that on that date the old woman of the woods let the cuckoo out of her basket (locally there used to be Cuckoo Fairs). For the last twenty years or so my children have given me cuckoo flowers on my birthday and it is a very rare year when there are none around by 14 April. This year I got a bunch on Mother's Day, 13 March!' (East Sussex, 1994)[20]

But in 1994 at least, correspondents showed that in many other parts of Britain, the first full blooming of the cuckooflower was a fairly accurate predictor of the first hearing of the bird itself:

	Cuckooflower	Cuckoo
Farnham, Surrey	10 April	21 April
Dymock, Glos.	15 April	24 April
Lugwardine, Hereford	21 April	25 April
Cutnall Green, Worcs.	23 April	24 April
Upton-by-Chester, Ches.	24 April	29 April
Kidlington, Oxon.	27 April	28 April
Gt Houghton, Northants.	21 April	1 May
Shrewsbury, Shrops.	29 April	1 May
Forest of Ae, Dumfries	30 April	4 May
Gourock, Renfrewshire	6 May	8 May[21]

Danish scurvygrass, *Cochlearia danica*, used to be confined, like most of its relatives, to coastal habitats, and to a few inland railway-line sites, where its seeds are believed to have been introduced with ballast from the seashore. But in the late 1980s it began to appear along the edges of major roads, almost always on the central reservation. By 1993 there were colonies on stretches of motorway and trunk roads in 320 10-kilometre squares. There are now concentrations on, for example, the M4, M5 (especially around Cardiff and Cheltenham), M6 and M56, along many reaches of the A1, the A5 in Anglesey, the A11 in Suffolk and the A30 in Devon, and on dual carriageways around Christchurch and Poole in Dorset. It has even crossed the Scottish border and appeared on the A74 in Dumfriesshire.

On many roads it seems to be spreading at the rate of some 10 to 15 miles per year, and rapidly builds up continuous colonies many miles long. In March and April, its profusion of low-growing, small white flowers can look like a layer of hoar-frost on the edge of the central reservation.

There can be little doubt that the turbulence caused by fast-moving traffic is what is wafting its seeds along at such a remarkable rate, and that the bare, stony edges of trunk-road verges (often liberally doused with spray from de-icing salt) are a congenial habitat for this native of maritime shingle banks.

Danish scurvygrass, rapidly colonising the edges of motorways and trunk roads.

But its preference for central reservations is still a puzzle (though it seems to be becoming less pronounced the more the species spreads around the road system). It may be partly a consequence of the greater speed of traffic along the lanes nearest the central reservation, the more powerful slipstream and spray they create, and the better drainage of the raised (usually) central reservation.[22]

Mountain avens, *Dryas octopetala*, is an exquisite mat-forming arctic-alpine that has probably been continuously present in Britain since before the Ice Age. It must have

Mountain avens was probably widespread after the last glaciation, but it is now confined to mountainous areas in the north and west.

been widespread immediately after the retreat of the glaciers, but is now confined to calcium-rich rock-ledges and crevices in mountainous areas in the north and west, especially in Snowdonia, the Lake District and the western Highlands. The flower is pure white, but seems to have a sheen, reflected from the dense central cluster of golden stamens. The seed-head that follows is a feathery sheaf, twisted at the top as if it were a sweet-wrapper.

*Cow parsley:
humbly named, but
no other plant gives
so much character
to country roads in
May.*

D. octopetala, as its name suggests, usually has eight petals. But doubles are quite frequent, and in the Burren in Ireland, where the limestone pavements are covered by sheets of the flower in May, the botanist Mary-Angela Keane has seen an individual with 17 petals.

Cow parsley, *Anthriscus sylvestris* (VN: Queen Anne's lace, Lady's lace, Fairy lace, Spanish lace, Kex, Kecksie, Queque, Mother die, Mummy die, Step-mother, Grandpa's pepper, Hedge parsley, Badman's oatmeal, Blackman's tobacco, Rabbit meat). Cow parsley is arguably the most important spring landscape flower in Britain. For nearly all of May, almost every country road is edged with its froth of white blooms. Regions where bluebells are embattled in private woods and buttercups sprayed out of the fields are still ornamented by mile upon mile of this indomitable, dusty smocking. It is odd that its rather dismissive English name – which simply means (in reference to the leaves) an inferior version of real parsley – has stood out against all comers. Queen Anne's lace sometimes makes a bid to replace it but has never become widely used, despite no end of elaborate stories to explain its origin as a name:

'Queen Anne's Lace is so called I understand because when Queen Anne travelled the countryside in May the people said that the roadsides had been decorated for her.'[23]

'The story is that Queen Anne, who suffered from asthma, used to come out to the countryside around Kensington, then open meadow and farmland, to get fresher air. As she and her ladies walked along the country lanes in spring sunshine, they carried their lace pillows and made lace. The flowering cow parsley, with its beautiful, lacy flowers, resembled the court ladies' lace patterns, and so the country folk began to call it Queen Anne's Lace, a name which persists today.'[24]

'Queen Anne's Lace is generally understood to refer to its lace-like appearance, but also to her (Queen Anne's) tragic child losses.'[25]

All the explanations have a rather contrived feel about them, and it is more likely that the name is an import from North America, where cow parsley is widely naturalised. A Warwickshire woman's experience lends wry circumstantial evidence to this possibility: 'At the Warwickshire Trust gift shop where I work as a volunteer, we sell silver pendants

and brooches containing pressed wild flowers. One morning two Alaskan men came into the shop, and selected pendants containing tiny white flowers on a black background
– very striking. The problem came when they wanted the
name of the flower. It was cow parsley. They were doubtful
if this would convey the right message to Alaskan women.
We ventured the alternative name of Queen Anne's Lace
(hoping we were right). Big smiles. The flowers immediately looked *much* prettier and we had two satisfied customers.'[26]

At any rate Queen Anne's lace hasn't caught on, and perhaps the unpretentious 'cow parsley' is the best name for
this truly vernacular blossom. It certainly has not dimin-
ished its rising reputation as a decorative flower. The sprays
work very well in a vase, looking spacious and balanced,
and keeping both their shape and blossom for more than a
week. They are becoming popular in church decoration,
too;[27] and I have seen them used in the flower arrangements
for a May wedding at Selborne, Hampshire.

The old dialect term 'kex', which has several derivatives
(see above), is still in use, but it is also applied to other umbellifers, including hogweed and hemlock, and especially to
the dried stalks of these plants. Its origins are unknown.

'Mother die' remains the most widely current – or at
least most remembered – alternative name, the implication
being that if you pick the plant your mother will die. Perhaps this is guilt by association, resulting from the slight
similarity between the scents of cow parsley and may, to
which a similar superstition is attached. But several potential victims have suggested that for them it is simply a useful
warning tag, which they have passed on to their children to
discourage the picking of *any* umbellifers – a family full of
deceptively similar edible and toxic species. Just how con-
fusing the family can be is illustrated by this story from
Yorkshire, of cow parsley and pignut being taken for the
same species: 'When I was a child we used to dig for hours
(with penknives) underneath "Mother Die" plants, otherwise known as Queen Anne's Lace. If we were *very* lucky,
we found something resembling an oddly shaped nut – a
"cat nut" – which was similar in taste to hazel nut or celery.
Incidentally I have dug under Mother Die this year, but
never found the delicious cat nut of childhood.'[28]

Germander speedwell, once worn by travellers as a good-luck charm.

Properly identified, in fact, young cow parsley leaves (it is a relative of the herb, garden chervil, *A. cerefolium*, which occurs occasionally as an escape) are a fresh and mildly aromatic addition to salads and omelettes.

Germander speedwell, *Veronica chamaedrys* (VN: Bird's eye, Cat's eye, Eye of the child Jesus, Farewell, Goodbye). Speedwells are roadside plants which speed you on your journey. Just why they acquired this reputation is unknown, but in Ireland they were sometimes sewn onto the clothes of travellers for good luck. In the eighteenth century they acquired another odd reputation, for curing gout, and 'Sir' John Hill reported that 'the dried leaves picked from the stalks, were sold in our markets, and the people made tea of them. The opinion was so prevalent, that the plant was in a manner destroyed for many miles about London, but, like all other things that want for truth for their foundation, it came to nothing.'[29]

Germander speedwell has bright blue flowers with white 'bird's eyes' and can often form large clumps in hedgebanks and open woodlands. The nineteenth-century flower painter Caroline May found a pink-flowered variety in Breamore, Hampshire, and an off-white one in South Petherwyn, Cornwall.[30] I have seen a single plant with pale grey flowers on a laneside bank at Hawkley in Hampshire.

Daisy, *Bellis perennis*. There is a saying that spring has not arrived until you can cover three, or nine, or a dozen daisy flowers with your foot. If there is some disagreement about the requisite number, it is because there is scarcely a day in the year (except during freezing weather) when there is not a daisy in flower somewhere. In his Journal for 1824, John Clare notes that he 'gatherd a hand ful of daiseys in full bloom' on Christmas Day.[31]

In the short turf of paddocks and lawns they can grow in constellations so dense that there is no space between the flowers, and it is this sheer availability and abundance that is partly responsible for their popularity in children's games.

Seven daisies underfoot. Enough for spring?

These go some way beyond the familiar daisy chain, made by threading the wiry stalks through each other, via slits made with a fingernail. In Wales there is a custom of making daisy 'caterpillars': 'We used to make caterpillars by taking a daisy with a long stem and then threading more daisy heads onto that. This was done by pushing the head of the first daisy (the long one) through the yellow part of the daisy heads.' [32]

A variant on threading games was the manufacture of inverted – 'Irish' or 'Australian' – daisies:

'An Irish daisy is one where the head has been turned upside down and re-threaded on its stalk, making it look as if it has grown with the head the wrong way round.' [33]

'This is how to make an Australian daisy. Pick a daisy. Pick the stem as low as you can, right next to the flower. There will be a sort of covered hole where the stem was. Stick the stem back through the hole till it comes through the yellow disc florets.' [34]

In Clwyd children play a game with daisy heads reminiscent of the flicking or 'flirting' games played with cigarette cards (or milk-bottle tops when 'fag-cards' were scarce).[35] This is an account by a 12-year-old girl:

'We used to play a game called Flacks in primary school. We would use a lot of daisy heads to make a circle, filled. Then we would throw dandelion heads into the circle and see how many flowers you could hit in the circle. The flowers which you did you won. The one with the most daisies won!' [36]

'We made daisy chains and also daisy plaques, using mud on old plates and sticking the heads in patterns. Although we knew and saw well-dressing in the Peak District I don't remember using any flower except daisies.' [37]

Recognising daisies as attractive flowers despite their humble status is probably an adult response, and William Hazlitt in his lecture 'On Thomson and Cowper' suggests: 'The daisy that first strikes the child's eye in trying to leap over his own shadow, is the same flower that with timid upward glance implores the grown man not to tread on it.' [38]

'The down-to-earth nature of the daisy has penetrated the language, where "daisy roots" is now slang for "boots" and "kicking up the daisies" a term used to describe those who have given up earthly gardening once and for all.' [39]

But the name is quite unequivocal in its affection. It is, as Chaucer wrote in the best tribute to the daisy, the day's-eye, which opens with the dawn and reflects the sunrise in the pinkish flush on the underside of its petals:

The yellow flag, the commonest native iris.

> *Now have I thanne eek this condicioun,*
> *That, of al the floures in the mede,*
> *Thanne love I most thise floures white and rede,*
> *Swiche as men callen daysyes in our toun.*
> *To hem have I so gret affeccioun,*
> *As I seyde erst, whanne comen is the May,*
> *That in my bed ther daweth me no day*
> *Than I nam up and walkyng in the mede*
> *To seen this flour ayein the sonne sprede …*
> *And lenynge on myn elbowe and my syde,*
> *The longe day I shoop me for t'abide*
> *For nothing elles, and I shal nat lye,*
> *But for to loke upon the dayesie,*
> *That wel by reson men hit calle may*
> *The 'dayesye,' or elles the 'ye of day,'*
> *The emperice and flour of floures alle.*
> *I pray to God that faire mote she falle,*
> *And alle that loven floures, for hire sake!*[40]

Yellow iris, *Iris pseudacorus* (VN: Yellow flag, Segg, Jacob's sword). Common by streams, rivers and ponds, and in fens, ditches and damp meadows throughout Britain, this is a robust plant, and the yellow flowers, out from mid-May, are one of the great spring ornaments of wetlands. It is sometimes suggested as the origin of the 'fleur-de-lis' of heraldry. 'Segg' (a variant of 'sedge') is from the Anglo-Saxon for a short-sword, a reference to the blade-like character of the leaves.

Spring crocus, *Crocus vernus* (VN: Nottingham crocus), and **autumn crocus**, *C. nudiflorus*. Towards the middle of the nineteenth century the flood meadows of the River Trent to the south of Nottingham were covered in March with the soft lilac spears of spring crocuses. It was a spectacular display that supported something close to a local festival:

'This harbinger of the vernal season is at the present moment enlivening the Nottingham meadows with

thousands of its purple blossoms. Hundreds of "young men and maidens, old men and children" may be seen from the Midland Railway picking the flowers for the ornamentation of their homes. Any stranger fond of flowers who visited Nottingham now for the first time would feel surprised to see large handfuls of Crocuses in the windows of the poorer and middle-class inhabitants. Crocuses in mugs, in jugs, in saucers, in broken teapots, plates, dishes, cups – in short, in almost every domestic utensil capable of holding a little fresh water; and very beautiful they look, even amidst these incongruities, still they look far fresher when seen nestling among the fresh green herbage of these oft-inundated meadows.' (1872) [41]

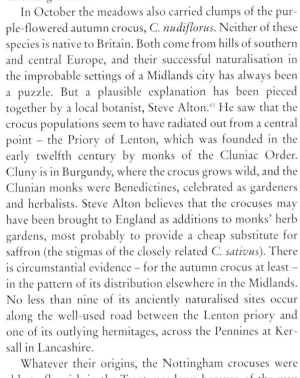

But by the 1970s, its colonies were greatly reduced: 'In 1974, I went to visit a friend who lived at Nuthall, about five miles from Stapleford. He showed me a pot of spring crocus which had come from an old lady's garden. This lady had originally dug up the plants from the meadow areas of Nottingham. In the 1970s the crocus was found growing in the General Cemetery, Beeston Field Golf Course, The Old Bramcote Church grounds, and Moorgate Congregational Church grounds.'[42]

In October the meadows also carried clumps of the purple-flowered autumn crocus, *C. nudiflorus*. Neither of these species is native to Britain. Both come from hills of southern and central Europe, and their successful naturalisation in the improbable settings of a Midlands city has always been a puzzle. But a plausible explanation has been pieced together by a local botanist, Steve Alton.[43] He saw that the crocus populations seem to have radiated out from a central point – the Priory of Lenton, which was founded in the early twelfth century by monks of the Cluniac Order. Cluny is in Burgundy, where the crocus grows wild, and the Clunian monks were Benedictines, celebrated as gardeners and herbalists. Steve Alton believes that the crocuses may have been brought to England as additions to monks' herb gardens, most probably to provide a cheap substitute for saffron (the stigmas of the closely related *C. sativus*). There is circumstantial evidence – for the autumn crocus at least – in the pattern of its distribution elsewhere in the Midlands. No less than nine of its anciently naturalised sites occur along the well-used road between the Lenton priory and one of its outlying hermitages, across the Pennines at Kersall in Lancashire.

Whatever their origins, the Nottingham crocuses were able to flourish in the Trent meadows because of the way they were managed. They were 'Lammas land' – hay meadows 'shut up' to allow grass to grow between Candlemas (2 February) and midsummer; then again between Old Lammas Day (13 August) and 3 October: 'It so happened that while the fields were closed to allow the hay to grow … the spring crocus flowered, produced its leaves and set seed. In addition, the autumn crocus produced leaves and perhaps small amounts of seed. While the fields were closed in August and September, to allow the grass to grow for

Spring crocus in Nottingham, where it has been naturalised since the Middle Ages.

Green-winged orchid, a declining species of damp, short, undisturbed grassland.
Bratoft Meadows, Lincolnshire.

winter grazing, the autumn crocus flowered. It is this fortunate compatibility between the traditional management of
British meadows and the life-cycle of Central European
crocuses that allowed the two species to flourish and spread
for hundreds of years.'[44]

This century, they have fared less well. Many of the sites
have been developed or flooded. The autumn crocus has a
site in a more remote Trent valley meadow, but seems to
have left the city itself. But *C. vernus* has clung on, and
keeps a tenuous link with its past. There is a colony on the
Nottingham University campus, close to the former site of
the Priory Grange of Farnstead (part of the priory demesne,
which may have had its own herb garden). Steve Alton
believes the small colony in the General Cemetery (see
above) may be a remnant of a much larger population which
grew all over 'the Forest' – a large area of open space which
hosts the annual Goose Fair. This area was formerly known
as the Sand Field, and was one of the chief areas of grazing
land around the city. When the Burgesses of Nottingham
removed their livestock from the Lammas meadows down
by the Trent, they moved them to the Sand Field. The crocus corms may well have been transported there stuck to the
feet of cattle. The Sand Field was divided up in 1865 to give
various areas of public open space (including a cemetery).

In Lancashire, Allan Marshall has done an independent
study of the sites of the autumn crocus, and reached a similar conclusion – though in this case the agents of distribution seem to have been the Knights of the Order of St John
of Jerusalem, returning from the Crusades. All the per-
suasively 'wild' sites of autumn crocus in the county – at
Middleton, Chadderton, Crompton, Oldham, Milnrow,
Healey, Rochdale Milhouse and Hollingworth – are on
land owned by the Knights of St John Hospitallers in the
thirteenth century.[45]

Elsewhere in Britain both spring and autumn crocus are
quite widely naturalised in churchyards, parks and road-
sides, the latter being the most thoroughly established
(though fine displays of *C. vernus* can be seen at Inkpen in
Berkshire and at Ellen Willmott's old garden, now a nature
reserve, in Essex). Other species that occasionally escape
and naturalise include the lavender-flowered **early crocus**,
C. tommasinianus, **Kotschy's crocus**, *C. kotschyanus,* and

Bieberstein's crocus, *C. speciosus* (both pale mauve with dark outside veining), which occur in churchyards and along waysides in Surrey and Suffolk.[46]

And in a wide grass verge alongside Church Lane, Tottenham, Brian Wurzell has found a remarkable colony of crocuses – anciently planted, of course, but now thoroughly established – which includes not only most of the species above but also a 'hybrid swarm' made up of crosses between the pale lilac *C. biflorus* and the yellow *C. chrysanthus*. He has distinguished at least ten varieties – including pure white flowers; a form with white segments above and dark purple 'birds' wings' pencilled below; and a dusky hybrid with mixed yellow and lilac flowers.[47]

Green-winged orchid, *Orchis morio*, is somewhat like a small early-purple orchid (see p. 66), but the 'hood' of the flower is shot through with delicate green veining. It is a declining species of undisturbed short grassland, especially damp meadows. It made an unexpected (and unprecedented) appearance 'at short mid-wicket' on the cricket ground at Stansted Park in West Sussex in May 1992.[48]

Rites of Spring

'Every year on Good Friday we would set off after lunch (boiled cod), each with our basket and a good stock of small balls of wool, for the woods, where we would sink down on the mossy grass and pick bunch after bunch of primroses to decorate the Priory Church on the next morning for Easter Sunday. If Easter was late the woods would be full

of the sound of cuckoos and perhaps we might even see a swallow … White violets had their Special Places. The ones I remember best were at the base of the old flint walls round the churchyard or by the footpath to the Goodwood Dairy which we passed along weekly to fetch our two pounds of butter …' (M. K. Farmer, Petersfield, Hampshire)

'The Vuz Dance of Flowers', a spring 'trade dance' revived in West Torrington, Devon in 1994.

'**Spring festivals**'. To say that most spring ceremonies and traditions involve plants would be true, but would be to miss the point: the encouragement and celebration of new growth – both wild and cultivated – is what these ceremonies are for. They are, to use that much misused phrase, fertility rites.

A surprisingly large number survive in modern Britain, yet because of religious, political and commercial pressures they have tended to coalesce around a few key dates, pagan quarter days and Christian festivals merging for convenience with twentieth-century bank holidays. The sacred and secular elements become blurred in a similar way. Only one occasion has no ceremonials attached to it and that, ironically, is the most 'natural' of all – the spring equinox of 21 March, optimistically called 'the first day of spring'.

One key historical factor must be taken into account in considering the match between the dates of various festivals and the 'natural' calendar. Up until the mid-eighteenth century two different calendars had been operating simultaneously in Britain, the 'Old Style' Julian calendar and the 'New Style' Gregorian calendar. In 1751, Lord Chesterfield's Act provided that the Gregorian calendar should become the norm throughout Great Britain and its dominions. By this time the discrepancy between the Old and New Styles had reached 11 days and, to normalise affairs,

Wild flowers used for a children's Easter flower arrangement in Okeford Fitzpaine, Dorset.

Meadow saxifrage and cow parsley in a well-dressing arrangement at Monyash, Derbyshire.

Parliament decreed that the days between 2 and 14 September 1752 should be omitted. From then on, natural events were tagged with a calendar date of 11 days later. So, if primroses traditionally flowered on 21 March in a village, they now bloomed on April Fool's Day.

The various species associated with spring festivals are discussed under their individual entries, but the following are some of the chief festivals that involve plants.

The Christian festival of Eastertide begins with Palm Sunday, when sprays of pussy willow or yew are sometimes used as substitutes for true palm. Primroses have become the flower of Easter itself and are often used to decorate churches.

May Day is the occasion of the old Celtic festival of Beltane, which is echoed in dozens of ceremonies across Britain: in Padstow, Cornwall, cowslips are worn in the Obby Oss procession; in Oxford, a Jack-in-the-Green cloaked in hawthorn leaves careers through the city. 'May birching' is largely obsolete, but involved fixing sprigs of plants to people's doors. The plants were chosen either because of their symbolic associations or because their names rhymed with the epithet regarded as most apt for the householder. So, plum, holly or briar meant, respectively, glum, folly or liar.[1] May garlands are still made on May Day in many country schools (and, more traditionally, in a few villages). At Charlton-on-Otmoor, there is a belief that the local May Day garland ceremony is an almost thoroughly Christianised relic of an old pagan festival. The Rector writes:

'With the coming of Christianity the missionaries had two choices with this, as with other customs – they could suppress it or adapt it. It would seem that they adopted the second course. It was clearly impossible to continue a pagan spring festival, so that ended; instead a Christian festival was held in honour of the Blessed Virgin Mary. This was, or became, associated with the figure on the rood in the church, representing the Lord's Mother. With the coming of Christianity, therefore, the pagan mother-goddess was no longer worshipped … It is a traditional custom, from time immemorial in the village, that children make little crosses covered with flowers … Since 1963 they bring them in procession to the church, where a service takes place, followed by dancing in the village street. The verse makes it clear that [the carol they sing] relates not to the May garlands carried by the children, but to the decorated "garland" on the north end of the screen, which indeed stood "at the Lord's right hand".'[2]

The Garland King, covered in flowers and foliage, like a Green Man, is carried on horseback throughout the Garland Day celebration in Castleton, Derbyshire, on 29 May.

The more secular garland ceremony at the Oxfordshire village of Bampton has, ironically, migrated to the more overtly Christian festival of Whitsuntide. The flowers used in what is a partly competitive ceremony must be wild: 'The fields belonging to the old Busby brothers were filled with every flower you could think of – Moondaisies, Harebells, Goozie Ganders, Pots and Pans, Clovers, Ragged Robins and Quaker Grass. We picked yellow flags from the brook, because these went on the top of the garland. The flowers were usually kept in a tin bath until Sunday evening. To make the garlands, two willow sticks were tied in circles and placed one inside the other, tied at the top. The grown-ups, mainly Mums, would then tie the flowers (which by this time we had bunched in small bunches) in identical order up each side of the hoops. When all the sides were covered, the garland would be hung on the line, splashed with water and left till morning.'[3]

Other festivals which doubtless began as May Day rites for encouraging growth in fields and woods have also moved towards the end of the month, often joining the civic commemoration of the Restoration of Charles II on 29 May (e.g. Oak Apple Day and Grovely, and Arbor Day at Aston on Clun). Rather more have clustered around the movable feast of Rogationtide (the fifth week after Easter, leading up

to Ascension Day). Rogation Sunday became officially sanctioned by the Church for the blessing of crops, which was combined with the social business of reaffirming land boundaries and common rights in the ceremony known as Beating the Bounds or Perambulation. Plants were invariably involved in this, being amongst the most frequent natural features marking boundaries, as well as instruments (in the form of elm or willow wands) for beating them. The seventeenth-century poet and populist preacher George Herbert, Rector of Bemerton in Somerset, listed the benefits of the ceremony, including 'a blessing of God for the fruits of the field; Justice in the preservation of bounds; Charitie in living walking and neighbourly accompanying one another'.[4]

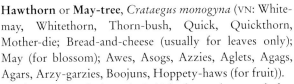

Hawthorn or **May-tree**, *Crataegus monogyna* (VN: White-may, Whitethorn, Thorn-bush, Quick, Quickthorn, Mother-die; Bread-and-cheese (usually for leaves only); May (for blossom); Awes, Asogs, Azzies, Aglets, Agags, Agars, Arzy-garzies, Boojuns, Hoppety-haws (for fruit)).

A descendant of the original Christmas-flowering 'Glastonbury Thorn' on Windmill Hill, Somerset, with Glastonbury Tor in the background.

The May-tree is the only British plant to be named after the month in which it blooms and seems to have acquired its eponymous title some time in the sixteenth century. Its blossoming marks the cusp between spring and summer, and the old saw 'Cast ne'er a clout ere May is out' almost certainly refers to the opening of the flowers, not the end of the month. It was the ancestor of the Maypole, the source of May Day garlands and the decoration of Jacks-in-the-Green and Green Georges, and one of the models for the foliage which wreathes the faces of Green Men carved in churches and inns. Superstitions about the flowers – and especially about the dire consequences of bringing them inside the house – persist more widely than for any other species. Isolated hawthorns are treated with respect, too, and, though often little more than bushes, are the most frequent trees mentioned in Anglo-Saxon boundary charters. The thorn is also the tree after which the Anglo-Saxon runic letter þ is named. It is a formidable list of honours for a tree which these days is often written off as 'scrub'.

There are some obvious reasons for the attention which was paid to hawthorn historically – the combination of thorns and red berries, for instance, which suggested a tree associated with protection and sacrifice, perhaps even the source of Christ's crown of thorns. The blossom too – white, heavy, sweet-and-sour, 'the risen cream of all the milkiness of May-time' as H. E. Bates put it[5] – must always have been cheering after a dark winter.

Yet these features hardly explain such an extravagant history of veneration. Why should a small, commonplace and not especially long-lived tree have been so often chosen to mark boundaries and meeting places? How could its blossom be so festively flourished at spring ceremonials, yet be banished from houses? How did a shrub that seems to bloom most typically in middle and late May become the symbol of May Day itself, the beginning of the whole cycle of spring festivals?

This last anomaly is perhaps the easiest to explain. Before

Hawthorn blossom, 'the risen cream of all the milkiness of May-time' (H. E. Bates).

the revision of the calendar in 1752, which did away with 11 days (see p. 118), May Day occurred on what, in the modern (Gregorian) calendar, became 12 May. This is the kind of date on which hawthorn customarily breaks into bloom today, so it is a fair assumption that, for all but the last two centuries, may blossom would have begun opening on May Day – at least in the warmer south and west of Britain. W. G. Hoskins put the current date for the Midlands as 18 May: 'On that day these miles of snowy hedges reach perfection, so dense and far-reaching that the entire atmosphere is saturated with the bitter-sweet smell whichever way the summer wind is blowing.'[6]

This evocative description of the Midlands fieldscape highlights another crucial change in the status of hawthorn. Those endless, single-species quickthorn hedges simply did not exist before the great parliamentary enclosures of the eighteenth and nineteenth centuries, in which something like 200,000 miles of thorn hedge were planted. Before that, hawthorn was a frequent (rather than abundant) component of mixed-species hedges and of chalk scrub, fens and woodland clearings. In blossom-time it was isolated individuals and clumps that would have shone out in the landscape, not the billowing ribbons which we see today.

But hawthorn is notoriously erratic in its flowering, and greatly influenced by late winter and spring temperatures. A contributor who has recorded its first flowering regularly in Minehead, Somerset, found that over the period 1984 to 1994 this swung between the extremes of 19 April (1989) and 26 May (1987).[7] Its flowering is also influenced by altitude, soil, shade, and these days by provenance (many of the earliest leafing and flowering specimens are from a cultivated variety introduced for hedging from the Netherlands). On the first two days of May 1994, for example, the first may blossom was recorded in Minehead, Somerset; Burgess Hill, West Sussex; Rayleigh, Essex; Much Marcle, Herefordshire; Cresswell, Staffordshire; and Tadcaster, North Yorkshire.[8] More revealing was Judith Allinson's meticulous account from Yorkshire, relating the first blooming of the may to altitude. At 60 m near Leeds, the flowers were just appearing on 16 May; at 100 m (Skipton) on 23 May; at 316 m (Cowside, near Settle) on 16 June; but not until 24 June at 345 m on the same hill. At 388 m, near

Double hawthorn, painted by James Sillett, 1803.

Hawthorn.

Ja. Sillett. 1803.

Malham Tarn, the first bushes did not begin to flower until the beginning of July and one was still in flower on 29th.[9]

The general coincidence that existed formerly between the flowering of the may and May Day itself, the Celtic festival of Beltane, might begin to explain the tree's reputation. Yet it has never generated an unqualified welcome for may flowers. Although the blossom has been used profusely for garlands and open-air decoration, there is still a widespread superstition (respected, if not literally believed – like that of walking under ladders) that may blossom is unlucky inside a house, and likely to presage a death:

'When I was teaching in Warwickshire, a child brought in a bunch and her class teacher seized them between her finger and thumb and flung them out through the window. (However Proust describes the church in Combray, and particularly the altar, being decorated with May for the Virgin.)'[10]

'As children in North Wales we never took branches of this tree into the house as it was meant to cause the death of your mother – I assume because of the suffocating smell the blossoms have in a closed room. Its Welsh name is "Blodau marw mam", literally "Flowers-death-mother".'[11]

'When I married my former husband in 1973 and moved to a Tudor house in the village of Denton, Kent, he immediately removed a hawthorn tree from the garden due to a superstition handed down the generations to him. This is interesting as his background is as follows. His great-grandfather emigrated from Scotland in 1885, having been a farm labourer. He was aged 21 years. My husband was a fourth generation New Zealander who came back to the UK in the 1960s bringing this superstition with him.'[12]

All kinds of reasons and rationalisations are given for the superstition. The flowers formed the wreaths worn by human sacrifices during the Celts' spring fertility rituals (a myth for which there is no historical evidence whatever). The pollen sparks off hay fever, or aggravates spring chest disorders. The white flowers, with their red anthers and incipient red berries, suggest blood and the pallor of corpses. (Red and white flowers together are still unpopular in hospitals.)[13]

Many contributors (mostly Catholics themselves) were taught that the superstition had its roots in the era of

Catholic suppression in Britain. A Benedictine nun writes: 'My mother, who was brought up in Aberdeenshire of Orcadian stock, was not especially superstitious, but held that it was unlucky to bring hawthorn into the house. May is associated with Our Lady and I wonder whether it might be an anti-Catholic connection. My mother was a non-Catholic. I also understand the superstition does not exist in Ireland.' [14]

'I was brought up in Kent in the 1920s, and there the reason given for not bringing May into the house was that it had long been seen as the Virgin Mary's plant, so if you took it into the house you might be thought to be a papist.' [15]

'Before the Reformation, when England was Catholic and known as Our Lady's Dowry, people used to make in their homes, during the month of May (the month dedicated to Mary and bearing her name), "May Altars", that is to say they would set up in a prominent place a statue of Mary, and surround it with flowers, particularly hawthorn, May, which was flowering in abundance. During and after the Reformation, with the imposition of the new form of worship and Puritanism, such acts were forbidden by law so that anyone being seen taking such decoration into their homes was immediately branded "Papist" and subject to heavy fines, imprisonment and, in some cases, death. You may like to know that Catholics still make their "May Altars" without worrying about any superstitions attached to the May.' [16]

'When I was at boarding school in North Yorkshire in the 1940s, I was told that the old superstition of it being unlucky to bring May into the house dated from the custom of Catholic recusant families of placing a sprig of May blossom in the window to indicate that a priest would be saying Mass there, a practice which was forbidden in those post-Reformation times.' [17]

Yet Marina Warner, in her book on the cult of the Virgin Mary, argues that the association between the month of May and Mary began only in the eighteenth century in Italy, from whence it spread to the rest of the Catholic world. [18]

A more immediately plausible reason for the superstition is that the triethylamine responsible for the stale element in hawthorn's complicated smell is one of the first chemicals produced when living tissue starts to decay. In some areas it is still believed to be 'the smell of the Great Plague'.[19] Nurses who have worked in Africa say it is reminiscent of the smell of gangrene. Perhaps its malign associations simply echo the time when corpses were kept at home for up to a week before burial, and people were much more familiar with the smell of death. (Ted Hughes bluntly describes may blossom's smell as that 'aniseed, corpse odour'.)

Yet triethylamine's fishy scent is also the smell of sex – something rarely acknowledged in folklore archives, but implicit in much of the popular culture of the hawthorn. The Cambridge anthropologist Jack Goody suggests that this may be the reason for the different degrees of tolerance of may blossom inside and outside houses: 'The hawthorn or may was the special object of attention at May Day ceremonies that centred on the woods, the maypole and the May queen … In contrast to Christmastide greenery and Easter willow, it is a plant kept outdoors, associated with

Hawthorn leaves and fruit carved in the Chapter House at Southwell Minster.

unregulated love in the fields rather than conjugal love in the bed.'[20]

There is some circumstantial evidence for this in the *doubles entendres* of a May Day folk-song still remembered in some Hertfordshire families:

> *We've been rambling all this night*
> *And the best part of the day,*
> *And now we're returning back again*
> *We've brought you a branch of May.*
>
> *Arise, arise you pretty fair maids*
> *And take your May Bush in,*
> *For if it's gone before morning comes*
> *You'll say we've never been.*
>
> *I have a purse upon my arm,*
> *It draws with a silken string,*
> *And all it wants is a little silver*
> *To line it well within.*[21]

It may be common hawthorn's preference for open country (in contrast to woodland hawthorn), for heaths and rocky places for example, that also helped make it such a significant boundary tree. Historically, hawthorn seems to have been *noticed* more than any other species. In his survey of 658 Anglo-Saxon charters and boundary descriptions Oliver Rackham found that it is, by a considerable margin, the commonest tree mentioned as a feature, representing 38.7 per cent of all trees specified. (Oak is next with 13.1 per cent.)[22] It also heads the list of trees mentioned in English place names, with 18 per cent.

Hawthorn is customarily thought of as an ephemeral tree, springing up on ungrazed commons or downland to form a brief, scrubby presence before 'proper' woodland supersedes it. In practice, thorn thickets or 'spinneys' (from the Latin *spinetum*) can be remarkably resilient, and reluctant to give way to other types of woodland, as on some of the clay-with-flint commons of the Chilterns. A particularly long-lived spinney is on the Dry Tree Barrow on Goonhilly Down, Cornwall, which is named as *cruc draenoc* ('thorny barrow') in a Saxo-Cornish perambulation of AD 977.[23] Perhaps many of the boundary thorns in charters were persistent, self-perpetuating groves of thorn, rather than individual trees.

Vaughan Cornish, who suspected there was a Belgic or Romano-British thorn-cult in early Britain, traced several specific landmark thorns or thorn clumps, at, for instance, Spelthorne in Middlesex, Shimpling Thorn in Norfolk, and his own village of Salcombe Regis in Devon.[24] Here, a memorial stone by the current tree carries this inscription: 'A thorn tree has been maintained here since Saxon times when it marked the boundary between the cultivated field of the coombe and the open common of the hill. It has given the name Thorn to the adjacent house where the Manor Court was held and to the surrounding farm. Vaughan Cornish, Christopher Tomkinson, Trustees of the Thorn Estate.'[25]

Near Bracon Ash in central Norfolk, there is a boundary and meeting-place thorn which is believed to be at least 700 years old. The Hethel Old Thorn, or Witch of Hethel, close to the isolated Hethel Church, is mentioned in a thirteenth-century charter. In the mid-eighteenth century, Robert Marsham, one of Gilbert White's correspondents

Hawthorn is an opportunist shrub, beginning woods wherever it is protected from grazing.

and a great lover of trees, found that its girth was more than 20 feet.[26]

The most celebrated old hawthorn is the Holy Thorn at Glastonbury in Somerset, which produces flowers and young foliage in midwinter, as well as blossoming again at the normal time in May. (It is now conventionally regarded as a sport, *C. monogyna* 'Biflora'.) The tree is first mentioned in an anonymous early sixteenth-century poem entitled 'Here begynneth the lyfe of Joseph of Armathia'. The poem described three thorn trees growing on Weary-All Hill, just south of Glastonbury, which

> *Do burge and bere greene leaues at Christmas*
> *As freshe as other in May when ye nightingale*
> *Wrestes out her notes musycall as pure glas.*

But an explicit connection between the thorns and St Joseph of Arimathea was not made in print until the seventeenth century. Then a variety of explanations – some based on theological argument, others on oral tradition – began to surface. Local legend had it that Joseph was an uncle of the Virgin Mary and had come to Britain with 11 other disciples some time between AD 30 and 63. He had travelled to Glastonbury and had thrust his staff in the ground, where it took root and grew to become the original Christmas-flowering thorn. A variant of the story suggested the tree sprang miraculously from a fragment of Christ's Crown of Thorns, brought to Britain by Joseph; another that the second blossoming coincides with Easter, so that the two flowerings symbolically encompass the whole of Christ's earthly existence. (It is quite possible that the tree was brought from the Middle East at some time, as there are Mediterranean populations of *C. monogyna* that do put out blooms in early winter.)[27]

During the sixteenth and seventeenth centuries pieces of the thorn were repeatedly cut off, either as souvenirs or as cuttings to grow on. In one way this was fortunate, as the Glastonbury tree received a more drastic and eventually fatal hacking from the Puritans, who abhorred idolatry, especially of trees. But a cutting was soon established in its place, as were similar cuttings all over England. There have been notable and long-established Glastonbury scions at, for instance, Quainton and Shenley (both Bucking-hamshire) and at Houghton-le-Spring, Tyne and Wear – the 'Gilpin Thorn'.[28]

After the calendar change of 1752, the trees were the subject of widespread superstitious attention, to see if they would bloom according to the old or the new calendar. Roy Vickery documents many examples of huge gatherings at the trees, stretching into the early years of this century, including a crowd of more than 2,000 at Quainton on Old Christmas Eve, 4 January 1753.[29] These days the blossoming of the trees is extremely variable, sometimes, after a mild autumn, as early as November, sometimes not until early March if there is a severe winter. But each year, just before Christmas, sprays from one of the thorn trees which grows in St John's churchyard in Glastonbury are sent to the Queen and the Queen Mother. The Queen is said to place hers on her breakfast table on Christmas morning.[30]

In the village of Appleton, Cheshire, what is presumed to be a descendant of the Glastonbury Thorn is still dressed with red ribbons and flags at midsummer. 'Bawming the Thorn' ('bawming' is a local dialect word meaning adorning or anointing) has clear affinities with other pre-Christian tree ceremonies. But the official tradition is that it commemorates the planting of a Glastonbury Thorn scion by Adam de Dutton on his return from the Crusades in 1125. For a supposedly 'holy' thorn it has had a rather luckless history. What was probably a second-generation successor was blown down in 1965. Its replacement quickly withered and died, and was replaced two years later. The Bawming ceremonials have been erratic, too, and were suppressed during Victorian times because they became too rowdy. Originally they took place on Old Midsummer's Day (5 July), but recently they have tended to be held on a Saturday close to the new Midsummer's Day in June.[31]

In the 1990s, a self-sown Christmas-flowering thorn (20 feet high) was discovered on Saltwells Local Nature Reserve in the West Midlands, which rather supports the theory that it is a naturally occurring sport of the native race of common hawthorn.[32]

There are other landmark thorns, both sacred and secular: 'A lone hawthorn, by the side of a rough track near Kilmeford, Argyll, is the local equivalent of a wishing well, with coins hammered into the bark.'[33]

'In 1811, at the time of the Napoleonic Wars, Selkirk Town Council agreed to billet French prisoners of war. They were housed in a crow-stepped building now used as the town library. The prisoners had a lenient incarceration, perhaps due to "the Auld Alliance". They had the freedom to walk as far as "the Prisoners' Bush", about two miles distant. The bush was a hawthorn. Sadly it became frail and was blown down about 18 months ago [1993] but it has been replaced by another hawthorn which is growing well.'[34]

Some old thorn hedges and individual trees have been pressed into domestic use: 'In our village till recently, there was a double hawthorn hedge, planted on a bank with a path between the hedges, which years ago was used for spreading linen on to dry.'[35] In the Isle of Man hawthorn bushes are sometimes trimmed to shape in order to hold milk pails while they are drying.[36] A tree at Ravenshead in Nottinghamshire is shaped in the form of a table top.[37] Hawthorn is the symbol of West Bromwich Albion Football Club: 'When the site was developed in 1900, the area was full of hawthorn bushes, and these in turn were full of thrushes. The locality was known as The Hawthorns. The stadium took its name from the same source, and also adopted the thrush (known locally as the throstle) as part of its crest.'[38]

Young hawthorn leaves are often the first wild green leaves that children eat, and they are universally known as 'bread and cheese'. This is usually explained as referring to their rudimentary culinary qualities. But some children have eaten the berries (whose flesh is a little like overripe avocado pear or, more fancifully, a whey cheese) together with the autumn leaves. These are just about edible, even in early October, and are certainly no worse than very stale bread: 'We would pick the red berries and green leaves in the autumn. These were known as "bread and cheese" – the leaf the bread, the berry the cheese.'[39] A more interesting use of the young leaves is the recipe given to Dorothy Hartley by a farm labourer's wife in Wymeswold, Leicestershire, in the 1930s. It was a 'spring dinner', made by covering a suet crust with young hawthorn leaf-buds and thin strips of bacon, and rolling and steaming as a roly-poly.[40]

Source notes

SELECT BIBLIOGRAPHY

Bates, H. E., *Through the Woods*, 1936
Clare, John, *The Midsummer Cushion*, Ann Tibbles (ed.), 1978
Cornish, Vaughan, *Historic Thorn Trees in the British Isles*, 1941
Gerard, John, *The Herball*, 1597
Goody, Jack, *The Culture of Flowers*, 1993
Greenoak, Francesca, *God's Acre*, 1985
Grigson, Geoffrey, *The Englishman's Flora*, 1955 and 1987
Hole, Christina, *British Folk Customs*, 1976
Mabey, Richard, and Evans, Tony, *The Flowering of Britain*, 1980
Rackham, Oliver, *Ancient Woodland*, 1980
Rackham, Oliver, *The History of the Countryside*, 1986
Vickery, Roy (ed.), *A Dictionary of Plant Lore*, 1995

NOTES

Woods

1 Gilbert White, *The Natural History of Selborne*, 1789
2 Martin Cragg-Barber, Chippenham, Wilts.
3 Mrs Cawthorne, Stanton, Suff.
4 Jonathan Spencer, 'Indications of antiquity. Some observations on the nature of plants associated with ancient woodland', in *British Wildlife*, 2 (2), 1990
5 K. Martin, Stanley Common, Derby.
6 J. E. Smith and J. Sowerby, *English Botany*, 1790–1814; 3rd edn, Boswell Syme (ed.), 1849–54
7 William Robinson, *The Wild Garden*, 1870
8 Revd W. Keble Martin and Gordon T. Fraser (eds), *Flora of Devon*, 1939
9 H. J. Riddelsdell *et al.*, *Flora of Gloucestershire*, 1948
10 J. W. and Anne Tibble (eds), *The Poems of John Clare*, 1935
11 Oliver Rackham, *Hayley Wood: Its History and Ecology*, 1975
12 Mark Powell, Riseley, Beds.
13 Gerard, 1597
14 Dorothy Mountney, Harleston, Norf.
15 C. A. Sinker *et al.*, *Ecological Flora of the Shropshire Region*, 1985 and 1991
16 John Raven and Max Walters, *Mountain Flowers*, 1956

17 Mrs Seeley, Catton, Northum.
18 Richard Mabey and Francesca Greenoak, *Back to the Roots*, 1983
19 A. J. Showler and T. C. G. Rich, '*Cardamine bulbifera* … in the British Isles', in *Watsonia*, 19(4), 1993
20 John Prince, Milton Keynes, Bucks.
21 P. Mead, Kingston St Mary, Somer.
22 Richard Mabey (ed.), *The Frampton Flora*, 1985
23 John Evelyn, *Acetaria: A Discourse of Sallets*, 1699
24 Dorothy Gibson, Carnforth, Lancs.
25 Michael Braithwaite, Hawick, Roxburghshire; Ida Turley, Ty Gwyn, Clwyd
26 Vita Sackville-West, *The Land*, 1926
27 Grigson, 1955
28 Gerard, 1597
29 Philip Oswald, 'The Fritillary in Britain. A historical perspective', in *British Wildlife*, 3(4), 1992
30 Douglas H. Kent, *The Historical Flora of Middlesex*, 1975; J. Blackstone, *Fasciculus Plantarum circa Harefield sponte nascentium*, 1737
31 Derek Wells, Hilton, Cambs.
32 Ruth Ward, Culham, Oxon.
33 *ibid.*
34 Andrew Young, *A Prospect of Flowers*, 1945
35 E. Duffey *et al.*, *Grassland Ecology and Wildlife Management*, 1974
36 Grigson, 1955
37 Leonard Bull, Bainbridge, N. Yorks.
38 A. T. Woodward, Stone, Bucks., per Peter Knipe, Dorchester, Oxon.
39 Elizabeth Evans, Kinoulton, Notts.
40 G. T. Hartley, *Some Notes on the Parish of Lapley-cum-Wheaton Aston*, per Ken Harris, Wheaton Aston, Staffs.
41 Caroline Smedley, Newton Regis, Staffs.
42 F. W. Simpson, 'Mickfield Fritillary Meadow, East Suffolk', in *SPNR Handbook*, 1938
43 C. Henry Warren, *Content with What I Have*, 1967
44 Mabey and Evans, 1980
45 Philip Oswald, *op. cit.*
46 Jean Kington, Leyburn, N. Yorks.
47 Goronwy Wynne, *Flora of Flintshire*, 1993
48 Clare, 1978
49 *The Journals and Papers of Gerard Manley Hopkins*, ed. H. House, completed by G. Storey, 1959
50 Francesca Greenoak, Wigginton, Herts.
51 Caroline and Peter Male, Halesowen, W. Mids
52 Ruth Ward, Culham, Oxon.

53 Helen Proctor, Upper Dicker, E. Susx
54 Jane Thompson, Markfield, Leics.
55 Joan Lancaster, Bletchley, Bucks.
56 Martin Jenkins and Sara Oldfield, *Wild Plants in Trade*, 1992
57 F. H. Perring, in *BSBI News*, 69, 1995; *Bluebell Signs on British Inns*, BSBI report [1994]
58 Margaret Gelling, *Place Names in the Landscape*, 1984
59 Colin Jerry, Peel, I. of M.
60 N. McArdle, Winterley, Ches.
61 John and Anna Taylor, Kirmond le Mire, Lincs.
62 Jane Halle, Romsey, Hants.
63 William Condry, *The Natural History of Wales*, 1981
64 Barbara Grover, Penzance, Corn.; also Pamela Michael, Lostwithiel, Corn.; Philip Hodges, Ewloe Green, Clwyd
65 Rackham, 1980
66 Gerard, 1597
67 Carolus Clusius, *Rariorum Plantarum Historia*, 1601
68 Revd W. Keble Martin and Gordon T. Fraser (eds), *op. cit.*
69 Chris Scott, Saltash, Corn.
70 Sean Street, *The Dymock Poets*, 1994
71 Mabey and Evans, 1980
72 Margaret and Bob Marsland, Hallwood Green, Dymock, Glos.
73 Dr Susan Warr, Mutley, Devon
74 Mr and Mrs T. M. Cave, Wiveliscombe, Somer.
75 Maggie Colwell, Box, Glos.
76 Ida Mullins, York; also Ursula Bowlby, New Forest, Hants.; Susan Cowdy, The Lee, Bucks.
77 Mike Coyle, Stoke, Devon
78 Trevor James, Hertfordshire Environmental Records Centre, Hitchin
79 E. Small, Washford, Somer.
80 G. Hurst, Bladford St Mary, Dorset
81 Doug Shipman, Broomfield, Essex
82 Michael Adey, Welling, Kent; A. Russell, Clevedon, Avon; Heather Hastings, Nutley, E. Susx; Doreen Farrant, Waldron, Heathfield, E. Susx; Rosemary Gilbert, Uckfield, E. Susx; E. Cole, Mayfield, E. Susx; Joan Dunlop, Staplecross, E. Susx; P. C. Mosby, Plummers Plain, Horsham, W. Susx; Deirdre Howe, Dial Post, W. Susx; Mary Middleton, Plaistow, W. Susx; Liza Goddard, Boundstone, Surrey; J. B. Haslam, Danhill Farm, Thakeham, W. Susx; I. MacDonald, Wiston, W. Susx

83 Alan Paine, Trimley St Mary, Suff.
84 Francis Simpson, *Simpson's Flora of Suffolk*, 1982
85 Dorothy Wordsworth, *Journals*, in *Home at Grasmere*, Colette Clark (ed.), 1960
86 Paul Jackson, Aberystwyth, Dyfed
87 David Jones, *The Tenby Daffodil*, 1992
88 *ibid.*
89 Charles Tanfield Vachell, *A Contribution Towards an Account of the Narcissi of South Wales*, 1894
90 T. A. Warren Davis, *Plants of Pembrokeshire*, 1970
91 Mabey and Evans, 1980
92 Grigson, 1955
93 Jocelyn Brooke, *The Wild Orchids of Britain*, 1950
94 Robin Ravilious, Chulmleigh, Devon
95 Margaret Trevillion, Germoe Churchtown, Corn.
96 John Ruskin, *Proserpina*, 1874–86

Primroses: First Flowers

1 Dorothy Gibson, Tunstall, Cranforth, Lancs.; also A. Dawson, Lochgilphead, Argyll.
2 Linda Ridgley, Warwickshire Rural Community Council, Warw.
3 Maureen Bayliss, Ollerton, Ches.
4 Christine Butcher, Holt, Wilts.
5 Lily Kelly, Handcross WI, W. Susx
6 Maggie Colwell, Box, Glos.
7 Margaret Trevillion, Germoe Churchtown, Corn.
8 Susan Cowdy, The Lee, Bucks.
9 J. Borough, Orleton, Shrops.
10 Rackham, 1980
11 P. Nash, Hele, Devon
12 T. Hull *et al.*, 'Primrose Picking in South Devon: The Social, Environmental and Biological Background', in *Nature in Devon*, 3, 1982
13 R. D'O. Good, 'On the distribution of the primrose in a southern county', in *Naturalist*, 809, 1944
14 Rackham, 1980
15 John Richards, University of Newcastle upon Tyne, in *BSBI News*, 60, 1992
16 H. M. Porteous, Leafields Farm, Shut Green, Staffs; also Jo Pasco, Tarewaste, Corn.
17 Gerard, 1597
18 Mrs Benyon, The Lee, Bucks.
19 John Ray, *Catalogus Plantarum circa Cantabrigiam nascentium*, 1660
20 J. E. Smith and J. Sowerby, *English Botany*, 1790–1814; 3rd edn, Boswell Syme (ed.), 1849–54

21 Henry Doubleday, in *The Phytologist*, 1, 1842; see also Stanley T. Jermyn, *Flora of Essex*, 1974
22 Mabey and Evans, 1980
23 Ian Hickling, Compton, Berks.
24 Susan Telfer, East Cowes, I. of W.
25 Anne Peyton, Lambley, Notts.
26 Roy Genders, *The Scented Wild Flowers of Britain*, 1971
27 Ian Hickling, Compton, Berks.

Lanes and Fields

1 Dr Larch Garrad, Manx Museum, Douglas, I. of M.
2 Mr Wilkinson, Clitheroe, Lancs.
3 Francis Simpson, *Simpson's Flora of Suffolk*, 1982
4 Margaret Grainger (ed.), *The Natural History Prose Writings of John Clare*, 1983
5 J. C. Lavin and G. T. D. Wilmore (eds), *The West Yorkshire Plant Atlas*, 1994
6 Gilbert White, *A Naturalist's Calendar ... ; extracted from the papers of the late Rev. Gilbert White M.A.*, J. Aiken (ed.), 1795
7 Henry Lyte, *A Nievve Herball*, 1578
8 Stephen Gill (ed.), *William Wordsworth*, 1984. 'To the Small Celandine' and 'To the Same Flower' were composed in the spring of 1802 and first published in *Poems in Two Volumes*, 1807
9 Frances Macdonald, Stratford upon Avon, Warw.
10 Barbara Penman, Hever, Kent
11 Grigson, 1955
12 Gerard, 1597
13 Jean Kington, Leyburn, N. Yorks.
14 Andrew Brockbank, Irby, Wirral, Ches.
15 Frances MacDonald, Stratford upon Avon, Warw.
16 Colin Jerry, Peel, I. of M.
17 Rosemary Reynolds, St Albans, Herts.
18 Mike Coyle, Stoke, Devon; Robin Ravilious, Chulmleigh, Devon
19 Grigson, 1955
20 Eva M. Cole, Mayfield, E. Susx
21 Bessie Hancock, Farnham, Surrey; M. Marsland, Dymock, Glos.; V. P. Helme, Lugwardine, Here.; E. A. Shuck, Cutnall Green, Worcs.; M. J., Upton-by-Chester, Ches.; Judith A. Webb, Kidlington, Oxon.; Alma Pyke, Great Houghton, Northants.; H. M. Edbrooke, Shrewsbury, Shrops.; Stan Farmer, Dumf.; A. MacLean, Gourock, Renfrewshire
22 Account based on contributions to *BSBI News*, 56, 64 and 65, 1990, 1993 and 1994, by

Nick Scott, Amble, Northum.; Trevor G. Evans, Chepstow, Gwent; Felicity Woodhead, Bournemouth, Dorset; and Simon J. Leach, Taunton, Somer.; with additional localities from Philip Oswald, Cambridge.
23 Carol Bennett, Sprowston, Norf.
24 Mrs Gibson-Poole, High Salvington, W. Susx
25 From Witham, Essex, May 1983, per Roy Vickery, in *BSBI News*, 69, 1995
26 Frances MacDonald, Stratford upon Avon, Warw.
27 Barbara Penman, Hever, Kent
28 N.M., Datchworth, Herts.
29 quoted in Vernon Rendall, *Wild Flowers in Literature*, 1934
30 Richard Mabey (ed.), *The Flowers of May*, 1990
31 Margaret Grainger (ed.), *op. cit.*
32 Seren Hathaway, Gwernaffield, Clwyd; also Hilary Foster, Sedbury, Gwent
33 S. A. Rippin, Fforest Coalpit, Gwent
34 John, Herne Bay, Kent
35 Iona and Peter Opie, *The Lore and Language of Schoolchildren*, 1959
36 Seren Hathway, Gwernaffield, Clwyd
37 E. Reeves, Sidcup, Kent
38 William Hazlitt, *Lectures on the English Poets*, 1819
39 Beryl Haynes, Handcross, W. Susx
40 Geoffrey Chaucer, Prologue to *The Legend of Good Women*, Text F, lines 40–8 and 179–87
41 *Gardeners' Chronicle*, March 1872
42 L. Sharp, Stapleford, Notts.
43 Steve Alton, Nottinghamshire Wildlife Trust
44 *ibid.*
45 Allan Marshall, Newhey, Lancs., in *BSBI News*, 58, 1991
46 Francis Simpson, *op. cit.*
47 Brian Wurzell, Tottenham, London, in *BSBI News*, 60, 1992
48 *The Times*, 13 May 1992

Rites of Spring

1 Hole, 1976
2 E. H. W. Crusha, Charlton-on-Otmoor, Oxon.
3 Ruth Wheeler, 'The wild flower garlands', in *The Bampton Beam*, April 1993; also Ruth Ward, Culham, Oxon.
4 George Herbert, *A Priest to the Temple*, 1652
5 Bates, 1936
6 W. G. Hoskins, *The Making of the English Landscape*, 1955
7 Caroline Giddens, Minehead, Somer.

8   *ibid.*; also M. Pearl Todd, Burgess Hill,
    W. Susx; Beryl Murfin, Rayleigh, Essex;
    Robert Hockley, Much Marcle, Here.;
    Dorothy Dixon, Cresswell, Staffs.; Margaret
    Fox, Tadcaster, N. Yorks.
9   Judith Allinson, Settle, N. Yorks.
10 Pauline Harris, Hagley, W. Mids
11 Anne Morris, Clwyd; also B. Bristow,
    Southport, Lancs.
12 Suzanne Royd-Taylor, Folkestone, Kent
13 Gillian Craig, Cambridge; Janie Clifford,
    Frampton on Severn, Glos.
14 Mother Mary Garson, Grace and
    Compassion Convent, Turners Hill, W. Susx
15 Veronica Holliss, Lumley, Hants.
16 Therise Christie, Folkestone, Kent
17 Sheila Dennison, Nympsfield, Glos.; also
    Dorothy Bell, Petts Wood, Kent; Peter
    Thornton, Eastwood, Notts.; C. M.
    Newman, Salisbury, Wilts.
18 Marina Warner, *Alone of All Her Sex*, 1978
19 Jennifer Westwood, Norton Subcourse,
    Norf.; also, Runcorn Hill Visitors' Centre,
    Ches.
20 Goody, 1993
21 Peter Rollason, Hitchin, Herts.
22 Rackham, 1986
23 Rackham, 1980
24 Cornish, 1941
25 Mavis Abley, Salcombe Regis, Devon
26 Cornish, *op. cit.*
27 Vickery, 1995
28 B. M. Fell, Quainton, Bucks.; Clare
    Mahaddie, Milton Keynes, Bucks.;
    H. Wilson, Houghton-le-Spring, Tyne and
    Wear
29 Vickery, 1995
30 *ibid.*
31 Cheshire Landscape Trust, Chester
32 Jim Beynon, Saltwells Local Nature Reserve,
    Dudley, W. Mids
33 Genevieve Leaper, Stonehaven, Kincard.
34 Elizabeth Telper, Selkirk, Borders
35 Ruth Watson, Haverfordwest, Dyfed
36 Dr Larch Garrad, Manx Museum, Douglas,
    I. of M.
37 J. A. Moulton, Ravenshead, Notts.
38 Dr John J. Evans, Secretary, West
    Bromwich Albion FC, W. Mids
39 Gwen Everitt, Torpoint, Corn.; also Mrs
    Gibson-Poole, High Salvington, W. Susx
40 Dorothy Hartley, *Food in England*, 1954

Acknowledgements

To the Countryside Commission, English
Nature, the Ernest Cook Trust and Reed Books
for so generously supporting the research stage
of the project.

To Common Ground – and Sue Clifford and
Angela King especially – who acted as charitable
host to the project and who were unfailing in
their support and encouragement whenever my
own enthusiasm showed signs of wilting. And to
Daniel Keech and John Newton, who worked as
full-time information and research officers,
principally from Common Ground's office, but
who also did invaluable and original fieldwork
beyond the call of duty.

To Peter Marren, James Robertson and Ruth
Ward, who co-ordinated research for us in
Scotland, Wales and Oxfordshire respectively.

To Roz Kidman Cox, editor of *BBC Wildlife*
Magazine, and Patrick Flavelle, producer of BBC
TV's *CountryFile*, who gave us space and time
(and encouragement) to recruit contributors.

To the many societies and associations,
national, regional and local, whose members and
staff were amongst the principal contributors:

Botanical Society of the British Isles, British
Bryological Association, British Association for
Nature Conservation, British Naturalists'
Association, British Trust for Conservation
Volunteers, Butterfly Conservation Society,
Churchyard Conservation Project, John Clare
Society, Council for Protection of Rural
England, Countryside Council for Wales,
Folklore Society, Forest Enterprise, Help the
Aged, Herb Society, Learning through
Landscapes, Local Agenda 21, National
Association for Environmental Education,
National Association of Field Studies Officers,
National Farmers' Union Scotland, National
Federation of Women's Institutes, National
Trust, Open Spaces Society, Plantlife, Poetry
Society, Ramblers' Association, the Royal
Botanic Gardens at Kew and Edinburgh, Royal
Forestry Society, Royal Society for Nature
Conservation, Scottish Environmental Education
Council, Scottish Natural Heritage, Tree Council
and the Parish Tree Wardens network, Watch,
Youth Hostels Association.

Arthur Rank Centre, Association of
Leicestershire Botanical Artists, Bioregional
Development Group, Bolton Museum, Cheshire
Landscape Trust, Cleveland Community Forest,
Cobtree Museum, the County Wildlife Trusts of:
Berkshire, Buckinghamshire and Oxfordshire;

Cambridge and Bedfordshire; Cleveland; Cornwall; Derbyshire; Gloucestershire; Hampshire and Isle of Wight; Hertfordshire and Middlesex; Kent; Lancashire; London; Norfolk; Northamptonshire; North Wales; Nottinghamshire; Scotland; Suffolk; Surrey; Wiltshire. Cymdeithas Edward Llywd, Derbyshire Ranger Service, Deeside Leisure Centre, Flora of Dunbartonshire Project, Groundwork Trusts of Merthyr and Cynon, Kent Thames-side and Amber Valley, Humberside County Council Planning Department, Liverpool Museum, Manchester Herbarium, Mid-Yorkshire Chamber of Commerce, Montague Gallery, Norfolk Rural Life Museum, Norfolk Society, North York Moors National Park, Social and Education Training Norfolk, Ted Ellis Nature Reserve, South-east Arts, University of Sussex Centre for Continuing Education, Warwickshire Rural Community Council, Wildplant Design.

Boxley Parish Council, Bradford City Council Countryside Service, Buchan Countryside Group, Thomas Coram School, Cumbria Broadleaves, Dragon Environment Group, Embsay with Eastby Nature Reserve, Giggleswick School, Great Torrington Library, Greenfield Valley Heritage Centre, Mike Handyside Wildflowers, Harehough Craigs Action Group, Hedingham Heritage Group, Hexham Nursery, Horsham Natural History Society, Ingleby Greenhow Primary School, Graham Moore Landscape Works, Lee Parish Society, Little Wittenham Nature Reserve, Oakfield Methodist Church, Paulersbury Horticultural Society, Pytchley Parish Sunday School Group, St Mary's Church Kirk Bramwith, Spiral Arts, Wealden Team Conservation Volunteers, West Bromwich Albion Football Club, White Cliffs Countryside Management Project, Whitegate and Marton Parish Council.

My personal thanks for their support to Charles Clark, Gren Lucas, Sir Ralph Verney and the late Sir William Wilkinson, and to the Leverhulme Trust for their generous award of a Research Fellowship to help fund my own researches.

To the friends and colleagues who gave me hospitality, company and much stimulating information during my own research trips: Elizabeth Roy and Nigel Ashby, Ronald Blythe, Hilary Catchpole and the pupils of Thomas Coram School, Berkhamsted, Rollo and Janie Clifford, David Cobham, Mike and Pooh Curtis, Roger Deakin, the late Edgar Milne-Redhead,

Robin and Rachel Hamilton, Anne Mallinson, Richard Simon, Jane Smart, Jonathan Spencer, Ian and Vicky Thomson. And to Liza Goddard, who acted as guinea-pig contributor whilst I was still refining the idea of the project and who accompanied me on some of the early field-trips, and to Pattie Barron for her patience.

To Penelope Hoare, my publisher at Sinclair-Stevenson, and the directors of Reed Books, who gave unflagging support to the project over what, in the modern book world, was a very long gestation period.

To Robin MacIntosh, my personal assistant, who helped in so many ways, especially with the awesome task of putting the contributions into some order. To Vivien Green, my agent, especially for bolstering me up during the low periods of the writing. To Douglas Matthews, for the speed and accuracy with which he produced the indexes. To Philip Oswald, whose vast background knowledge and meticulous attention to detail not only gave the text botanical respectability but added a wealth of anecdotes, historical notes and stylistic improvements. And to Roger Cazalet, my editor, for his diligence, dedication, patience and care.

And finally, the warm thanks of all of us go to the many thousands of people who contributed to *Flora Britannica* and without whom it would not exist. Those of you whose stories and notes have found their way into the text are individually acknowledged in the Source notes. But every single contribution helped form the entries and the overall flavour of the book. Please keep contributing, as we hope that the first edition of *Flora Britannica* will not mark the end of the project so much as the beginning of a new phase.

Index

Cutnall Green, Worcs., 99

Daffodil, 7, 53-61
  Tenby, 62-6
  van Sion, 65
Daisy, 106-8
Daisy-chains, 7
Dame's-violet, 84-5, 97
Dartington, Devon, 17
  Hall, 26
Dean Grove, Oxon, 48
Denton, Kent, 128
Derbyshire Dales, 16
Devil's Churchyard wood, near
  Checkendon, Oxon, 11
Dial Post, W. Susx, 61
Dickleburgh Fen, Norf., 79
Dinton (formerly Donnington),
  near Ford, Bucks., 37
Disraeli, Benjamin (Earl of
  Beaconsfield), 72
Ditchling Beacon, Susx, 70
Doctrine of Signatures, 89
Dog-violet
  Common, 17-18
  Early, 20
  Heath, 21
Donne, John: 'The Primrose', 69
Doubleday, Henry, 78
Dovedenhall Wood, Suff., 78
Druce, George Claridge, 32
  Flora of Oxfordshire, 48, 82
Dry Tree Barrow, Goonhilly
  Down, Corn., 131
Dryas octopetala, 101-3
Ducklington, Oxon, 33, 36
Dunsford, Devon, 61
Dutton, Adam de, 134
Dymock, Glos., 55-7, 60, 99

East Anglia, 23, 48-9, 69, 78, 79
Easter, 70, 97, 116, 119
Ebbw Vale, Gwent, 65
Edmund, King, 51
Elchin Wood, near Elsted, Kent,
  60
Elizabeth II, Queen, 134
Eranthis hyemalis, 13
Erysimum
  cheiri, 97
  linifolium, 97
Evans, J.E., 64
Evelyn, John, 29

Farmer, M.K., 117
Farndale, N. Yorks., 54, 57
Farnham, Surrey, 99
Farnstead Priory, Notts., 114
Festivals (Spring), 118-28
Fingest, Bucks., 26
Fitzgerald, Edward: Omar
  Khayyam, 87
Fleam Dyke, Cambs., 87

Ford, Bucks., 37, 39-40
Forest of Ae, Dumfries, 99
Four Oaks, Glos., 57
Fox, 'Queenie', 41
Fox Meadow, Framsden, Suff.,
  41-2
Framsden, Suff., 41-2
Frenchlands, Steyning, W. Susx,
  61
Fritillaria meleagris, 30-42
Fritillary, 30-42

Garland Day (19 May), 121
Garland King, 121
Garlic, Wild, 11, 51-3
Garnham family (of Monewden),
  65
Genders, Roy: Collecting
  Antique Plants, 83
Gerard, John
  on daffodil, 53
  on fritillary, 31
  on primrose, 76
  on sweet violet, 20-1
  on thrift, 93
  Herball, 45
Gibson, George, 78
Glastonbury, Somer., 122, 133-4
Golden Parsonage, Herts., 60
Goldingtons, Herts., 60
Good Friday, 116
Good, Professor Ronald, 73-4
Goody, Jack, 130
Goonhilly Down, Corn., 131
Goosegrass, 7
Gourock, Renfrewshire, 99
Gowbarrow Park, Ullswater,
  Cumb., 61
Grasmere, Westmor., 91
Great Bardfield, Essex, 78
Great Houghton, Northants., 99
Green Man (figure), 121, 123
Greenoak, Francesca, 55
Grieve, James, 24
Grigson, Geoffrey, 31, 37, 66, 93
Grovely Forest, near Salisbury,
  Wilts., 120

Harebell, 45-6
Harefield, Middx, 32
Harleston, Norf., 23
Hartley, Dorothy, 135
Hartley, G.T., 40
Hawkley, Hants., 105
Hawthorn, 123-35
Hayley Wood, Cambs., 20
Hazlitt, William: 'On Thomson
  and Cowper', 107
Healey, Lancs., 114
Heather, 7
Heathfield, E. Susx, 61
Hedges, 126
Hele paper mill, Devon, 72

Hellebore
  Green, 13
  Stinking, 12
Helleborus
  foetidus, 12
  orientalis, 13
  viridis, 13
Helpston, Northants., 87
Hemlock, 12
Henley Nap, Oxon, 82
Herb-paris, 43-5
Herbert, George, 122
Hesperis matronalis, 97
Hethel, Norf., 132
Heythrop, Oxon, 48
Hickling, Ian, 75, 79, 83
Highlands of Scotland, 102
Hill, 'Sir' John, 105
Hogweed, 11
Hollingworth, Lancs., 114
Holly, 7
Holy Island Priory, Northum.,
  94, 97
Hopkins, Gerard Manley, 29,
  46-8
Hopkinson, John, 89
Hornbeam, 26
Horse-chestnut, 8
Horsham, W. Susx, 61
Horsted Keynes, E. Susx, 49
Hoskins, W.G., 126
Hospitallers see St John of
  Jerusalem, Order of
Houghton-le-Spring, Co.
  Durham, 134
Hughenden, Bucks., 72
Hughes, Ted, 130
Hunworth, Norf., 50
Hyacinthoides
  hispanica, 51
  non-scripta, 45-51
  × H. hispanica, 51

Iffley Meadow, Oxon, 36-7
Inkpen, Berks., 114
Ionine, 20
Ipsden, Oxon, 49
Iris, Yellow, 108-9
Iris pseudacorus, 108-9
Isophenes, 7
Iver, Bucks., 24

Jack-in-the-Green, 119, 123
Jones, David, 62
Joseph of Arimathea, St, 133

Keane, Mary-Angela, 103
Kempley, Glos., 56-7
Kersall, Lancs., 111
Kidlington, Oxon, 99
Kilmelford, Argyll, 134
Kingston Wood, Cambs., 78
Kington St Michael, Wilts., 32